Experimental Philosophy

For Donovan and Theresa

Experimental Philosophy
An Introduction

JOSHUA ALEXANDER

polity

First published in 2012 by Polity Press
Reprinted in 2013

Polity Press
65 Bridge Street
Cambridge CB2 1UR, UK

Polity Press
350 Main Street
Malden, MA 02148, USA

ISBN-13: 978-0-7456-4917-7
ISBN-13: 978-0-7456-4918-4(pb)

A catalogue record for this book is available from the British Library.

Typeset in 11 on 13 pt Bembo
by Servis Filmsetting Ltd, Stockport, Cheshire
Printed in the USA by Edwards Brothers, Inc.

The publisher has used its best endeavours to ensure that the URLs for external websites referred to in this book are correct and active at the time of going to press. However, the publisher has no responsibility for the websites and can make no guarantee that a site will remain live or that the content is or will remain appropriate.

Every effort has been made to trace all copyright holders, but if any have been inadvertently overlooked the publisher will be pleased to include any necessary credits in any subsequent reprint or edition.

For further information on Polity, visit our website: www.politybooks.com

Contents

Acknowledgments   vi

Introduction   1

1 Philosophical Intuitions   11

2 Experimental Philosophy and Philosophical Analysis   28

3 Experimental Philosophy and the Philosophy of Mind   50

4 Experimental Philosophy and Philosophical Methodology   70

5 In Defense of Experimental Philosophy   89

Epilogue   109
Notes   114
References   135
Index   150

Acknowledgments

Nothing is written alone, and I have benefited from the comments and advice of a large number of friends and colleagues. Among them, some deserve special thanks: John Alexander, Cameron Buckner, Adam Arico, Chad Gonnerman, Jonathan Ichikawa, Joshua Knobe, S. Matthew Liao, Ronald Mallon, Jennifer Nado, Shaun Nichols, Mark Phelan, Stephen Stich, and Jonathan Weinberg. At some point during the writing of this book, each of these people shared an insight that shaped the book in some significant way; many of them shared many, perhaps sometimes without knowing it, and their contributions to the book are immeasurable.

I would also like to thank my wonderful editor, Emma Hutchinson, the members of her team, and two anonymous referees at Polity Press, as well as Brandon Nelson, who provided the artwork used on the front cover. In both style and substance, this book is better for the care that they gave.

Chapter 5 contains a proper part of my paper "Is Experimental Philosophy Philosophically Relevant?" (*Philosophical Psychology* 23, 377–389). Permission to reprint is gratefully acknowledged. The real price of any book is time; time spent writing that might otherwise be spent with family and friends. Without the love and support of my friends and family, this book would not have been possible. I hope that, especially in their eyes, the book proves to be worth the price.

Introduction

1. Experimental Philosophy: Setting the Scene

We ask philosophical intuitions – *what we would say* or *how things seem to us to be* – to do a lot of work for us. We advance philosophical theories on the basis of their ability to explain our philosophical intuitions, defend their truth on the basis of their overall agreement with our philosophical intuitions, and justify our philosophical beliefs on the basis of their accordance with our philosophical intuitions. This may not be all that we do and maybe not all of us do it. But enough of us do it, and often enough, that this way of thinking about philosophy has come, at least in certain circles, to be *the* way to think about philosophy.

On this way of thinking about philosophy, it should seem natural for philosophers to be interested in studying people's philosophical intuitions. Traditionally, this interest has taken the form of an introspective investigation of our own philosophical intuitions. Assuming that our own philosophical intuitions are appropriately representative, nothing more is needed. The problem with this approach is that the habit of assuming that our own philosophical intuitions are appropriately representative turns out to be a *bad* habit. It ignores our human tendency to overestimate the degree to which others agree with us (see, e.g., Fields & Schuman 1976, and Ross 1977) and fails to recognize that philosophers compose a rather distinctive group, determined not only by a shared educational history but also by a shared interest in certain kinds of questions and in certain ways of approaching those questions. A better approach is needed.

In recent years, *experimental philosophy* has emerged as an exciting new approach to the study of people's philosophical intuitions. Experimental philosophers apply the methods of the social and cognitive sciences to the study of philosophical cognition since these methods are better suited than introspective methods to the study of what people, especially *other* people, actually think. These methods not only provide us with better access to the relevant intuitions themselves, they can also provide us with insight into the psychological mechanisms that are responsible for them and their overall evidentiary fitness. In this way, experimental philosophy can both complement more traditional approaches to philosophical questions and help identify ways in which this approach should be reformed.

Experimental philosophy is a diverse movement and, in this book, we will focus on three of its different programs:

- *Experimental Philosophy and Philosophical Analysis*: What has traditionally interested philosophers about people's philosophical intuitions has been what these intuitions are supposed to be able to tell us about the world and ourselves. This view is most commonly associated with *philosophical analysis*. Philosophical analyses often involve arguments that move from claims about people's philosophical intuitions to claims about the truth or plausibility of specific philosophical theories. Sometimes these theories are about our concepts of things; sometimes they are about things themselves. Either way, the idea is that philosophical intuitions are supposed to be able to help us answer certain kinds of philosophical questions, and some experimental philosophers see themselves as making important contributions to this project. These experimental philosophers typically share with more traditional analytic philosophers the idea that philosophical intuitions provide us with important philosophical insight, but believe that we should employ methods better suited to the careful study of philosophical intuitions, namely, the methods of the social and cognitive sciences.

- *Experimental Philosophy and the Philosophy of Mind*: Some experimental philosophers think that what philosophical intuitions can tell us about ourselves is not limited to what they can tell us about our individual or shared concepts of things, arguing that our philosophical intuitions also provide us with important philosophical insight into the nature of our minds. These experimental philosophers are less interested in identifying the precise meaning of philosophical concepts than they are in identifying the factors that influence our application of these concepts. The goal is not to use our philosophical intuitions to help explain the meaning of our philosophical concepts, but to explain our intuitions themselves, and by doing so, to reveal something philosophically important about how our minds work and how we ordinarily understand the world.

- *Experimental Philosophy and Philosophical Methodology*: As it turns out, learning more about how our minds work and how we think about philosophical issues has yielded significant insights into the methods that we employ when doing philosophy, and has led some experimental philosophers to raise concerns about the role that intuitions play in philosophical practice. It turns out that different people have different intuitions, and that people's intuitions are sensitive to a range of things (e.g., ethnicity, gender, affectivity, and presentation order) that we neither expected nor perhaps wanted them to be. What makes this situation worse is that, because we know so little about the cognitive processes involved, we currently lack the resources needed to determine *whose* intuitions to trust and *when* to trust them. After all, evidential diversity calls for some method of adjudication, unexpected evidential sensitivity for some method of forecast, and unwanted evidential sensitivity for some method of prophylaxis. What is needed, then, is a better understanding of the cognitive processes involved in the production of our philosophical intuitions. By coming to better understand what intuitions are, where they come from, and what factors influence them, we can better understand what role they can play in philosophical practice.

There are other ways of dividing up the landscape, and some work in experimental philosophy does not fit neatly into any of these categories, but enough does that this topography will be a useful, if not entirely accurate or exhaustive, guide to the experimental philosophy movement. At any rate, it will be our guide.[1]

2. A Note on Scope and Coverage

Books like this one are often measured not only by what is covered, but also by what is not. Although still young, the experimental philosophy movement has already produced more than what can adequately be treated in a short introduction, and so there are certain sins of omission in what follows. A few of these deserve special mention, and some attention, however brief.

Experimental Philosophy of Consciousness

Recently, there has been an explosion of interest in the experimental philosophy of consciousness and, in particular, interest in the distinction between *phenomenal consciousness* (experience) and *non-phenomenal consciousness* (agency). A great deal of this interest has focused on our *folk psychological* understanding of what is required in order for something to count as capable of phenomenal consciousness (as capable, for example, of seeing red or feeling pain), and whether those requirements differ from what is required in order for something to count as capable of non-phenomenal consciousness (as capable, for example, of forming beliefs, desires, and intentions). The early results have been fascinating, and suggest not only a rather complicated relationship between folk attributions of phenomenal consciousness and folk attributions of non-phenomenal consciousness (Gray et al. 2007, Knobe & Prinz 2008, Arico 2010, Huebner et al. 2010, Sytsma & Machery 2010, Arico et al. 2011), but also that folk psychological attributions of phenomenal consciousness are associated with attributions of moral standing (Robbins & Jack 2006, Gray & Wegner 2009). While a picture of the folk psychology of consciousness is beginning to emerge, more work will be needed in the coming years to explain the precise nature of the relationship between folk psychological attributions of phenomenal consciousness and attributions of non-phenomenal consciousness, and the cognitive process or processes that support both kinds of folk psychological mental state attributions.

Moral Philosophy and Moral Psychology

It is hard to over-emphasize the excitement and controversy surrounding much of the recent empirical work in moral psychology. Recent work in moral psychology draws on both the empirical resources of the social and cognitive sciences and the traditional conceptual resources of philosophy in order to carefully examine how we think about moral and ethical issues. The results have been fascinating, calling into question not only more traditional ways of approaching these issues, but also a number of orthodox views in philosophical ethics.

Character and Situation

Moral philosophers have often maintained that people possess robust character traits that are responsible for much of our moral and ethical behavior. Our character is not always virtuous, and can be influenced by contextual factors, but it is our moral character that explains the overall pattern of our moral and ethical behavior. While popular among moral philosophers, this view has come under attack in recent years due to the influence of empirical work in moral psychology. It turns out that people behave quite differently in different contexts, and that even minor contextual differences can influence our moral and ethical behavior. (See, for example, Isen & Levin 1972, Darley & Batson 1973, and Milgram 1974.) John Doris (1998, 2002) and Gilbert Harman (1999) argue that empirical findings spell trouble for character-based virtue ethics, arguing instead for a view they call *situationism*, according to which our moral and ethical behavior is determined not by robust character traits but instead in large part by contextual factors. (For recent discussions of the situationist challenge, including attempts to defend character-based virtue ethics, see Kupperman 2001, Sreenivasan 2002, Annas 2003, Kamtekar 2004, Appiah 2008, and Machery 2010.)

Reason and Emotion

Philosophers have long debated the role that emotion plays in moral judgment. Recently, this debate has taken an empirical turn. Evidence from neuroscience, social and developmental psychology, and psychopathology all seem to point to the view that emotions are essential to morality. The upshot has been a renewed interest in the idea that moral judgments are influenced in some manner by emotions or sentiments (dispositions to have certain emotions in certain circumstances). Shaun Nichols (2004b), for example, has argued that moral judgments arise from the interaction between our affective responses to certain events and normative theories specifying which actions are wrong. Nichols contends that both components of moral cognition are necessary since normative theories prohibit certain actions that we don't judge to be morally wrong (e.g., norms of etiquette) and we can have strong affective reactions to events without thinking that moral transgressions have occurred (e.g., a child falling down and skinning her knee). While these two parts of moral cognition are distinct, they come together in *core moral judgments* – judgments that involve "sentimental rules" that prohibit certain actions that are independently likely to elicit strong negative affective responses.

Jesse Prinz (2007) advances an even stronger position about the relationship between emotion and moral judgment, which he calls *strong emotionism*. According to strong emotionism, both our moral concepts and moral properties themselves are essentially related to our emotional responses. Where Nichols thinks that there is a causal relationship between our emotional responses and our moral judgments, Prinz contends that the relationship is *constitutive*. (Actually, Prinz contends that moral sentiments are constitutive of both moral judgments and moral properties. This provides for the possibility that some moral judgment might not be accompanied by occurrent emotional responses.)

So there seems to be a strong causal or constitutive relationship between moral judgments and emotions or sentiments. This puts pressure on the idea, long popular in moral philosophy, that it is reason that plays an essential role in moral judgments. At the very least, it seems like we must make room at the moral table for our emotions and sentiments. But, the outlook for reason might not even be this good. Jonathan Haidt (2001) has suggested that emotion and sentiment play such a significant role in moral judgments that deliberative reason typically comes in only after the fact to provide *post-hoc* rationalization of those moral judgments. If this is right, then reason becomes nothing more than apologist to moral judgment.

Neuroethics

One of the most interesting developments in recent moral psychology involves the use of functional neuroimaging technology to study moral cognition. Functional magnetic resonance imaging (fMRI) technology allows scientists to examine what areas of the brain are active when people make moral judgments and, by virtue of this, to better understand the different cognitive processes that are involved in making those judgments. Joshua Greene, for example, has used fMRI technology to advance what he calls a "dual process" theory of moral cognition, according to which characteristically deontological judgments are associated with emotional neural processes and characteristically consequentialist judgments are associated with deliberative cognitive processes (see, e.g., Greene et al. 2001 and Greene 2008). One advantage of the dual process theory is that it helps us understand the *trolley problem*, that is, why we think that it is morally permissible to sacrifice the life of an innocent bystander in certain versions of the trolley case but not in others. Greene (2003, 2008) and Peter Singer (2005) have also used evidence from neuroscientific studies of moral cognition as part of a normative argument about which kinds of moral judgments should be employed in moral philosophy. They contend that we have good reason to discount characteristically deontological judgments; namely, deontological judgments are sensitive to morally irrelevant factors and are associated with cognitive processes that weren't evolutionarily selected to track moral facts. While this argument has proved to be rather controversial (see, e.g., Berker 2009), the idea that neuroscience can play some role in not only moral psychology but also moral philosophy is gaining more and more acceptance in both science and philosophy.

Moral Reflection and Moral Behavior

When asked to explain the value of philosophical education, philosophers often suggest among other things that thinking carefully about normative issues can have a positive effect on moral agency. The idea is that careful moral reflection improves moral behavior, and that this is the true value of moral education. It's a nice story, but there is reason to worry that it isn't true. If moral education improves moral performance, then we might expect professional ethicists to be models of moral agency and to behave better than non-ethicists. After all, they devote their professional lives to moral reflection and moral education, and presumably care deeply about morality itself. Yet, professional ethicists seem to be no more charitable (Schwitzgebel & Rust, forthcoming), politically conscientious (Schwitzgebel & Rust 2010), or courteous (Schwitzgebel et al., forthcoming) than non-ethicists, and even seem to be more likely to engage in certain kinds of morally objectionable behavior (Schwitzgebel 2009). This makes it difficult to sustain the idea that moral education truly is ameliorative in nature, and suggests that the value of moral education must be found elsewhere. (Interestingly, not only does empirical research suggest that professional ethicists aren't models of moral agency, it also suggests that philosophers might already have known this at some level. See, for example, Schwitzgebel and Rust (2009). This makes it difficult to explain how the story rehearsed at the beginning of this paragraph got told in the first place.)

Experimental Philosophy of Science

Finally, it is worth briefly mentioning some extremely interesting work in the experimental philosophy of science that is concerned with understanding how we understand key scientific concepts – concepts like *explanation* and *gene*, to pick just two.

Explanation

We want to understand the world, and this means at least in part being able to *explain* why some things happen and others don't. But, what does it mean to explain why something happened (or didn't), and why does it matter so much to us to be able to do so? Recent empirical work by Tania Lombrozo (2006, 2011, and Lombrozo & Carey 2006) has begun to shed light on both of these questions. It turns out that we seem to prefer functional explanations (explanations in terms of reasons, functions, and goals) and that, while we tend to think that there is something intrinsically valuable about being able to provide explanations, this feeling is best explained in terms of the instrumental value that explanations have in our daily and scientific lives. Being able to explain why something happens supports our more practical goals of prediction and control, and we are sensitive to the explanatory properties that are themselves responsible for the practical benefits. We value explanations with those properties precisely because those properties give rise to practical benefits, even when we aren't consciously aware that these properties are responsible for the practical benefits.

Gene

According to the "classical theory" of concepts, concepts are associated with sets of individually necessary and jointly sufficient characteristics. While some scientific concepts seem to fit this model, others don't. (The same, of course, is true for non-scientific concepts as well.) Instead, some scientific concepts are vague or ambiguous, acquiring specific meanings in the different scientific contexts in which they are used. Recent empirical work by Paul Griffiths and Karola Stotz (2006, 2007) suggests that *gene* is this kind of concept; what it means for something to be a gene depends at least in part on the specific scientific context in which the concept is being used. But, if the concept *gene* is heterogeneous, and its meaning changes from context to context, then it becomes important to be able to determine not only what different meanings are in play but also when a specific meaning is in play. This turns out to be no easy task, and requires careful empirical examination not only of the different scientific contexts in which the concept *gene* is used, but also the way the concept has evolved in the history of biology. What we find is a remarkable pattern of different meanings across different scientific contexts.

3. An Issue Set Aside

Before we begin, it is worth saying something briefly about whether experimental philosophy really is philosophy.[2] It has become somewhat fashionable to charge that it is not; that it is, instead, simply experimental psychology, or perhaps the psychology of philosophy. This charge usually comes packaged together with a story about what kinds of questions count as genuine philosophical questions and what kinds of methods can be employed when trying to answer these questions. The trouble with packaging the charge in this way is that it smacks of philosophical imperialism. Unless we adopt overly narrow and seemingly arbitrary standards, it is hard to sustain the idea that experimental philosophical questions aren't genuine philosophical questions, or the idea that the methods of the social and cognitive sciences aren't legitimate philosophical methods. The real problem isn't how the charge is packaged, however; it's the charge itself. To see why, let's suppose that experimental philosophy *is* experimental psychology. So what? Unless we adopt a strict division of intellectual labor that permits no overlap, the fact that experimental philosophy asks questions about human cognition that are often associated with experimental psychology and uses the methods of the social and cognitive sciences doesn't mean that it isn't approaching genuine philosophical questions using appropriate philosophical methods. Questions can have both psychological *and* philosophical significance, and methods can transcend traditional academic boundaries. So, what's going on here? I suspect that the charge is usually motivated by the worry that *some* genuine philosophical questions simply cannot be answered using the methods of the social and cognitive sciences. Fair enough, but this only means that not all philosophy is experimental philosophy. Quite right. What follows is the story of that part of philosophy that is.

1

Philosophical Intuitions

George Bealer does it. Roderick Chisholm does it a lot. Most philosophers do it openly and unapologetically, and the rest arguably do it too, although some of them would deny it. What they all do is appeal to intuitions in constructing, shaping, and refining their philosophical views.

Hilary Kornblith (1998)

1. Introduction

Philosophical intuitions play a significant role in contemporary philosophy. Philosophical intuitions provide data to be explained by our philosophical theories, evidence that may be adduced in arguments for their truth, and reasons that may be appealed to for believing them to be true. In this way, the role and corresponding epistemic status of intuitional evidence in philosophy is similar to the role and corresponding epistemic status of perceptual evidence in science.[1] Since experimental philosophy grows out of this way of thinking about philosophy, understanding experimental philosophy requires thoughtful and careful examination of the nature of philosophical intuitions and the role that they play in contemporary philosophy. As such, we begin at the beginning, with the story of philosophical intuitions and their role in contemporary philosophical practice.

2. Intuitions and Philosophical Practice

Philosophers are concerned with evaluating theories about such things as knowledge, justification, meaning, moral responsibility, and morally right action.[2] Is knowledge simply justified true belief? Is a belief justified just in case it is caused by a reliable cognitive mechanism? Does a name refer to whatever object uniquely or best satisfies the description associated with it? Is a person morally responsible for an action only if she could have acted otherwise? Is an action morally right just in case it provides the greatest benefit for the greatest number of people all else being equal? When confronted with these kinds of questions, philosophers often appeal to philosophical intuitions about real or imagined cases. We advance philosophical theories on the basis of their ability to explain our philosophical intuitions, and appeal to them as evidence that those theories are true and reasons for believing as such.

To get a better sense of how this works, let's look at some examples. For a long time, philosophers thought that knowledge was simply justified true belief. Not anymore. Edmund Gettier (1963) changed our minds by presenting two hypothetical cases involving a person who has deduced a true belief *q* from a justified *false* belief that *p* and, on that basis, formed a justified true belief that *q* that doesn't *seem* to count as knowledge.[3] Here's one of Gettier's cases:

Suppose that Smith and Jones have applied for a certain job. And suppose that Smith has strong evidence for the following conjunctive proposition:

(d) Jones is the man who will get the job, and Jones has ten coins in his pocket.

Smith's evidence for (d) might be that the president of the company assured him that Jones would in the end be selected, and that he, Smith, had counted the coins in Jones's pocket ten minutes ago. Proposition (d) entails:

(e) The man who will get the job has ten coins in his pocket.

Let us suppose that Smith sees the entailment from (d) to (e), and accepts (e) on the grounds of (d), for which he has strong evidence. In this case, Smith is clearly justified in believing that (e) is true.

But imagine, further, that unknown to Smith, he himself, not Jones, will get the job. And, also, unknown to Smith, he himself has ten coins in his pocket. Proposition (e) is then true, though proposition (d), from which Smith inferred (e), is false. In our example, then, all of the following are true: (i) (e) is true, (ii) Smith believes that (e) is true, and (iii) Smith is justified in believing that (e) is true. (Gettier 1963, p. 122)

Smith has the justified true belief that the man who will get the job has ten coins in his pocket. Yet, it doesn't *seem* that he knows this. Instead, it is supposed to be clear that Smith does *not* know that the man who will get the job has ten coins in his pocket even though his belief is both justified and true. (Usually, people think that what has gone wrong is that Smith doesn't have access to the appropriate truth-makers – or at least that what makes his belief justified is not what makes it true – and so he is lucky that his belief is true.) We are supposed to just *see* this, and this is supposed to count as sufficient evidence against the claim that a person knows that *p* just in case that person's true belief is justified.[4] If Smith is justified in truly believing that the man who will get the job has ten coins in his pocket without knowing that it is true, then knowledge simply cannot be merely justified true belief.

Philosophical intuitions play a similar role in discussions about the nature of epistemic justification. Consider, for example, the claim that a person's belief that *p* counts as justified just in case it is caused, or is causally sustained, by a reliable cognitive process. While many philosophers have found this claim quite attractive, most philosophers now agree that being caused, or causally sustained, by a reliable cognitive process isn't *sufficient* for a person's belief that *p* to count as justified. To see why, consider the following hypothetical case:

Suppose a person, whom we shall name Mr. Truetemp, undergoes brain surgery by an experimental surgeon who invents a small device which is both a very accurate thermometer and a computational device capable of generating thoughts. The device, call it a tempucomp, is implanted in Truetemp's head so that the very tip of the device, no larger than the head of a pin, sits unnoticed on his scalp and acts as a sensor to transmit information about the temperature to the computational system of his brain. This device, in turn, sends a message to his brain causing him to think of the temperature recorded by the external sensor. Assume that the tempucomp is very reliable, and so his thoughts are correct temperature thoughts. All told, this is a reliable belief-forming process. Now imagine, finally, that he has no idea that the tempucomp has been inserted in his brain, is only slightly puzzled about why he thinks so obsessively about the temperature, but never checks a thermometer to determine whether these thoughts about the temperature are correct. He accepts them unreflectively, another effect of the tempucomp. Thus, he thinks and accepts that the temperature is 104 degrees. It is. Does he know that it is? (Lehrer 1990, pp. 163–64)

Truetemp's temperature beliefs are caused by a reliable cognitive process, and yet it doesn't *seem* like he knows that it is 104 degrees. In fact, it is supposed to be clear that Truetemp does *not* know that it is 104 degrees, and this is supposed to put pressure on the idea that a person's belief that p is justified if it is caused by a reliable cognitive process. If Truetemp doesn't know that it is 104 degrees even though his true belief that it is was caused by a reliable cognitive process, then clearly something more is needed in order to justify our beliefs than the mere fact that they are caused by a reliable cognitive process. It may be necessary that they are, but it clearly isn't sufficient.

We've looked at two examples of the role that intuitions play in contemporary epistemology. Of course, the role of intuitions in contemporary philosophy is hardly limited to epistemology. Let's consider a widely discussed example from the philosophy of language. According to the descriptivist theory of reference, there is a description associated with every proper name. This description specifies a set of properties and an individual object is the referent of a given proper name just in case it uniquely or best satisfies the description; that is, just in case it possesses all of the properties, or possesses more of the properties than does any other object, that are associated with the proper name. By contrast, according to the causal theory of reference, a proper name is introduced into a linguistic community for the purpose of referring to a specific individual. The name then continues to refer to that individual so long as its uses are linked to that individual through a causal sequence of successive uses; that is, so long as one's use of that name to refer to that individual object has been acquired from someone else's use of that name to refer to that individual object and so on back to the point at which the name was first introduced to refer to that individual object.

Which view is right? Prior to the 1970s, most analytic philosophers were descriptivists, believing that names refer to those objects that uniquely or best satisfy the descriptions associated with them. This changed (at least for a time) with the publication of *Naming and Necessity* (Kripke 1980).[5] There, Saul Kripke provided a series of powerful arguments against the descriptivist theory. The most famous of these arguments begins by describing a person who says that Gödel is the man who proved the incompleteness of arithmetic. This person knows enough mathematics to be able to give an independent account of the incompleteness theorem, but all that this person knows about Gödel is that he was the man who proved the incompleteness of arithmetic. With this in mind, Kripke asks readers to consider the following hypothetical case:

> Suppose that Gödel was not in fact the author of this theorem. A man named 'Schmidt', whose body was found in Vienna under mysterious circumstances many years ago, actually did the work in question. His friend Gödel somehow got a hold of the manuscript and it was thereafter attributed to Gödel (pp. 83–84).

According to the descriptivist theory of reference, when our fictional protagonist says that Gödel is the man who proved the incompleteness of arithmetic, he is referring to Schmidt because it is Schmidt who uniquely satisfies the description associated with the name 'Gödel' (namely, the person who proved the incompleteness of arithmetic). Yet, it doesn't *seem* like he is referring to Schmidt; instead, it *seems* like the person is referring to Gödel (even if some of his beliefs about Gödel have turned out to be false). And, it is a strike against the descriptivist theory that it is at odds with this intuition. The fact that the descriptivist theory of reference tells us that the person is referring to Schmidt when it seems obvious to us that the person is referring to Gödel suggests that it is not the case that names refer to those objects that uniquely or best satisfy the descriptions associated with them. By contrast, the causal theory of reference successfully explains why it seems to us like the person is referring to Gödel: his use of the name is appropriately linked to the introduction of the name to refer to Gödel. The ability of the causal theory of reference to explain why it seems like the person is referring to Gödel suggests that reference is fixed by the initial act of naming and that later uses of a name succeed by being causally linked to this initial act.

In addition to playing a significant role in epistemology and the philosophy of language, philosophical intuitions also play a significant role in contemporary discussions about the relationship between free will and moral responsibility. For example, many arguments for incompatibilism, the view that free will and moral responsibility are incompatible with causal determinism, rely on the principle that a person is morally responsible for her actions only if she could have done otherwise. If it's true that a person is morally responsible for her actions only if she could have done otherwise, and causal determinism entails that, given the actual past and the laws of nature, we can only perform those actions that we do perform, then causal determinism is incompatible with moral responsibility. But is this principle, commonly referred to as the *principle of alternative possibilities*, true? Harry Frankfurt (1969) gives us reason to worry that it is not. Frankfurt has readers imagine a person named Jones who has decided for reasons of his own to perform some action, but who is then threatened by another person with a penalty (one so harsh that any reasonable person would submit to the threat) unless he performs precisely that same action. Jones is neither an unreasonable man who acts without considering the consequences of his actions nor a man who is "stamped by the threat" such that "[g]iven the threat he would have performed that action regardless of what decision he had already made" (Frankfurt 1969, p. 832). Instead,

> [t]he threat impressed him, as it would impress any reasonable man, and he would have submitted to it wholeheartedly if he had not already made a decision that coincided with the one demanded of him. In fact, however, he performed the action in question on the basis of the decision he had made before the threat was issued. When he acted, he was not actually motivated by the threat but solely by the considerations that had originally commended the action to him. It was not the threat that led him to act, though it

would have done so if he had not already provided himself with a sufficient motive for performing the action in question. (Frankfurt 1969, p. 832)

According to the principle of alternative possibilities, Jones is not morally responsible for his action because he could not have done otherwise. Yet, it *seems* like he *is* morally responsible for his action. Jones decided to perform the action before the threat was made, and he acted on the basis of this decision and not on the basis of the subsequent threat. But, if Jones is morally responsible for his action, then a person may be morally responsible for his actions even if it is impossible for him to do otherwise – particularly, when the circumstances that make it impossible for him to do otherwise don't actually cause him to act in the first place.

Let's look at one more example, this time from normative ethics. Many moral philosophers believe that it is morally impermissible to cause harm unless doing so is the unavoidable side effect of an action intended to bring about a morally good state of affairs. While it is permissible to bring about harmful side effects in the course of bringing about some morally good state of affairs, it is impermissible to bring about those same harmful effects as a *means* of bringing about that state of affairs. One reason moral philosophers have had for endorsing this view, which is commonly called the *doctrine of double effect*, is that it helps to explain why we respond differently to the following two hypothetical cases:

Trolley:
Suppose that you are the driver of a trolley. The trolley rounds a bend, and there comes into view ahead five track workmen, who have been repairing the track. The track goes through a bit of a valley at that point, and the sides are steep, so you must stop the trolley if you are to avoid running the five men down. You step on the brakes, but alas they don't work. Now you suddenly see a spur of track leading off to the right. You can turn the trolley onto it, and thus save the five men on the straight track ahead. Unfortunately . . . there is one track workman on that spur of track. He can no more get off the track in time than the five can, so you will kill him if you turn the trolley onto him. (Thomson 1985, p. 1395)

Transplant:
[I]magine yourself to be a surgeon, a truly great surgeon. Among other things you do, you transplant organs, and you are such a great surgeon that the organs you transplant always take. At the moment you have five patients who need organs. Two need one lung each, two need a kidney each, and the fifth needs a heart. If they do not get those organs today, they will all die; if you find organs for them today, you can transplant the organs and they will all live. But where to find the lungs, the kidneys, and the heart? The time is almost up when a report is brought to you that a young man who has just come into your clinic for his yearly check-up has exactly the right blood-type, and is in excellent health. Lo, you have a possible donor. All you need to do is cut him up and distribute *his* parts to the five who need them. You ask, but he says, "Sorry. I deeply sympathize, but no." (Thomson 1985, p. 1396)

The doctrine of double effect explains why it *seems* morally permissible to redirect the trolley but not to sacrifice the healthy patient. In the trolley case, we do not intend to kill one worker as a means to saving the other five. His death is the unavoidable side effect of an action intended to bring about a morally good state of affairs. By contrast, we do intend to kill the healthy patient in order to save the other patients. His death is the means by which we would bring about a morally good state of affairs. By stipulating that it is morally permissible to bring about harmful side effects in the course of bringing about morally good states of affairs, but not to use harmful means to bring about morally good ends, the doctrine of double effect makes sense of our intuitions about these two cases, and this counts in its favor.[6]

3. Philosophical Intuitions

Examples like these abound. In fact, philosophical intuitions play such a significant role in contemporary philosophical practice that George Bealer (1992, 1996a, 1998) has said that philosophical intuitions are part of "our standard justificatory procedure". Describing the evidential role played by philosophical intuitions in defense of the claim that knowledge is not merely justified true belief, Bealer (1996a) writes:

> Now at one time many people accepted the doctrine that knowledge was justified true belief. But today we have good evidence to the contrary, namely, our intuitions that situations like those described in the Gettier literature are possible and that the relevant people in those situations would not know the things at issue. This and countless other examples show that, according to our standard justificatory procedure, intuitions are used as evidence (or as reasons). (p. 122)

Bealer not only makes the descriptive, sociological claim that philosophical intuitions are in fact a standard part of our justificatory practices, he also argues for the normative claim that they *must* be. The normative claim is part of his famous argument for the incoherence of empiricism, whose basic idea is that empiricists cannot defend their own methodological commitments using any set of justificatory resources that don't include philosophical intuitions. Other philosophers have gone further than Bealer, claiming not only that philosophical intuitions are part of our standard justificatory procedure, but also that this fact is part of what makes philosophical methodology unique. For example, Janet Levin (2005) writes:

> Is knowledge justified true belief? Is causation merely constant conjunction? Is conscious experience nothing but neural activity of a certain kind? These questions, insofar as they concern the nature of things (rather than merely the structure of our concepts), are modal theses, and thus cannot be investigated purely by empirical means. Instead, or so philosophers have traditionally held, they are to be answered by consulting our philosophical intuitions; that is, those peculiarly compelling deliverances about possibilities that arise from a serious and reflective attempt to conceive of scenarios that stand as counterexamples to these claims . . . This procedure of rejecting or modifying theses in the face of intuitively convincing counterexamples has been characteristic, perhaps definitive, of philosophical argumentation throughout its history. (p. 193)

And, Alvin Goldman (2007) writes:

> One thing that distinguishes philosophical methodology from the methodology of the sciences is its extensive and avowed reliance on intuition. Especially when philosophers are engaged in philosophical "analysis", they often get preoccupied with intuitions. To decide what is knowledge, reference, identity, or causation (or what is the concept of knowledge, reference, identity, or causation), philosophers routinely consider actual and hypothetical examples and ask whether these examples provide instances of the target category or concept. People's mental responses to these examples are often called "intuitions" and these intuitions are treated as evidence for the correct answer. At a minimum, they are evidence for the examples' being instances or non-instances of knowledge, references, causation, etc. Thus, intuitions play a particularly critical role in a certain sector of philosophical activity. (p. 2)

But, what are philosophical intuitions? Answers vary, often reflecting different attitudes about how we should go about trying to answer this question. Some philosophers encourage us to consult our intuitions about intuitions; others recommend paying special attention to what they introspectively seem to be from the first-person point of view; and still others advise looking closely at what philosophers appeal to as intuitional evidence in practice.[7] As Jonathan Weinberg and Joshua Alexander (forthcoming) point out, these different approaches have produced a range of conceptions from *thin conceptions* that treat philosophical intuitions as rather generic kinds of mental states (or episodes), typically beliefs or inclinations to believe, to *thick conceptions* that place additional conditions on what kinds of mental states count as genuine philosophical intuitions. Let's look briefly at some of these conceptions.

The Doxastic Conception

Some philosophers think that intuitions are simply beliefs, or perhaps inclinations to believe.[8] David Lewis (1983) adopts this view:

Our "intuitions" are simply opinions; our philosophical theories are the same. Some are commonsensical, some are sophisticated; some are particular, some general; some are more firmly held, some less. But they are all opinions, and a reasonable goal for a philosopher is to bring them into equilibrium. (p. x)

And Peter van Inwagen (1997) agrees:

Our "intuitions" are simply our beliefs – or perhaps, in some cases, the tendencies that make certain beliefs attractive to us, that "move" us in the direction of accepting certain propositions without taking us all the way to acceptance. (Philosophers call their philosophical beliefs intuitions because 'intuition' sounds more authoritative than 'belief'.) (p. 309)

And, while we might question whether van Inwagen has accurately captured our motivation for singling out some of our beliefs as philosophical intuitions, Timothy Williamson (2007) has recently argued that there are good reasons for thinking of them in this way: more restrictive conceptions don't adequately capture all of what philosophers appeal to as intuitional evidence in practice, and more inclusive conceptions help insulate philosophical intuitions from the threat of skeptical challenge by making global intuitional skepticism less and less attractive.[9] Still, there are other reasons to worry that the doxastic conception is simply too thin: many philosophers want to say that there are important differences between philosophical intuitions and other kinds of mental states, and we might worry that the doxastic conception doesn't put us in a position to be able to mark these differences.[10]

The Phenomenological Conception

One way to mark the difference between philosophical intuitions and other kinds of mental states is to suggest that genuine philosophical intuitions have special phenomenological characteristics that are introspectively accessible aspects of intuitional experience. Philosophical intuitions strike us in a certain way, perhaps as subjectively compelling or as necessarily true. George Bealer (1998) adopts this view, arguing that philosophical intuitions are *intellectual seemings* that have the *appearance of necessity*.[11] We have the philosophical intuition that *p* when it seems to us that *p* is necessarily true. This means that intuitions aren't beliefs since we believe that certain propositions are true even when they *seem* to us to be false (think, for example, of the claim that one infinite set can be larger than another) and believe that other propositions are false even when they *seem* to us to be true (think, for example, of the claim that every property defines a set containing exactly those things that possess that property).[12] But more important, at least for present purposes, is that it also means that not all intuitions are created equal, and we can distinguish philosophical intuitions from other kinds of mental states by the fact that philosophical intuitions present their propositional contents as necessary.

While this conception has been tremendously influential, it has also been extremely controversial, with much of the controversy surrounding the claim that philosophical intuitions involve the appearance of necessity.[13] As Joel Pust (2000) points out, one problem is that many propositions that might seem to us to be necessarily true when we stop to think about their modal status might nonetheless never appear to us to be necessarily true simply because we never stop to think about such things. The idea is that whether or not a proposition appears to us to be necessarily true depends not only on features of the proposition, but also on whether those features catch our attention. And this leaves open the possibility that propositions that *would* seem to us to be necessarily true under the right circumstance never *actually* appear to us in this way simply because the circumstances are never right. The upshot is that whether or not we have the philosophical intuition that *p* is going to end up depending on what we are paying attention to at the moment, and this seems somewhat counterintuitive, at least to some philosophers. The most natural solution to this problem, of course, would be to weaken the requirement that philosophical intuitions present their propositional contents as necessary by saying only that they must do so when we stop to think about their modal status. But, as Michael Lynch (2006) and Kirk Ludwig (2007) point out, some philosophical intuitions *never* involve the appearance of necessity, not even when we stop to think about their modal status. If this is right, then merely modifying the requirement won't do. Instead, it seems like we must dismiss the requirement entirely, and admit that philosophical intuitions need not involve any appearance of necessity whatsoever. The problem with doing this, however, is it leaves us in the position of having to find some other way of distinguishing philosophical intuitions from other kinds of mental states.

The Semantic Conception

Some philosophers have attempted to do this by arguing that philosophical intuitions must have a specific kind of propositional content. Ernest Sosa (1998) provides a nice example of this approach, arguing that philosophical intuitions must have *abstract* propositional content. Sosa doesn't say precisely what this means, instead saying that he will rely on our working understanding of what it means for a proposition to be abstract, but he does provide some glimpse of what he means when he says that abstract propositions don't mention any concrete particulars – no particular persons, places, or things. (They can mention particular properties or relations.) The problem with this approach is that it is also too strict, again leaving out certain things that we want to count as philosophical intuitions.[14] To see this, we need to be careful to distinguish between philosophical claims and the intuitions that are used to evaluate them. Philosophical claims are abstract. We say things like knowledge is justified true belief, beliefs are justified just in case they are caused by reliable cognitive mechanisms, names refer to whatever objects uniquely or best satisfy the descriptions associated with them, and so on, and these claims make no specific mention of concrete particulars. But the philosophical intuitions that we use to evaluate these claims are very often *concrete*. We say that it seems to us that Smith doesn't know that the man who will get the job has ten coins in his pocket even though his belief is both justified and true, that Truetemp doesn't know that it is 104 degrees even though his belief is caused by a reliable cognitive mechanism, that 'Gödel' refers to Gödel even though Schmidt best satisfies the description associated with that name, and so on, and these philosophical intuitions *do* mention concrete particulars. The problem is clear. If philosophical intuitions must have abstract propositional content, then these aren't philosophical intuitions; but surely they are.

The Etiological Conception

The idea behind both the semantic and phenomenological conceptions was to try to locate something in the content or appearance of philosophical intuitions that could be used to set them apart from other kinds of mental states. The problem is that too much seems to get lost in the mix. These conceptions turn out to be too discriminating, leaving too much out in their effort not to let too much in. This has led some philosophers to suggest that what makes philosophical intuitions different from other kinds of mental states has to do with where they come from rather than what they are or what it's like to have them. Kirk Ludwig (2007) advances this view, arguing that genuine philosophical intuitions are judgments made only on the basis of *conceptual competence*. In the same spirit, Ernest Sosa (1998) suggests that philosophical intuitions are inclinations to judge based on *conceptual understanding*, George Bealer (1998) claims that philosophical intuitions are the product of *determinate concept possession*, and Antti Kauppinen (2007) argues that they are what *competent users* of the relevant concepts would say in *sufficiently ideal conditions* where their judgments are *influenced only by semantic considerations*.

The common theme is that we can distinguish philosophical intuitions from other kinds of mental states by looking at the contribution that conceptual competence plays in the formation of particular intuitive judgments. It turns out, however, that this is actually quite hard to do. As we will see in later chapters, it is no easy task to determine precisely what is part of our conceptual competence and what is part of our conceptual performance (Alexander et al. 2010a, 2010b). But even if we set this worry to the side, the fact remains that we need some way of identifying which intuitions have the appropriate etiological pedigree, and the problem is that the cognitive processes involved are typically *unconscious* (Henderson & Horgan 2000, 2001) or otherwise *introspectively opaque* (Lynch 2006). We may have privileged access to the contents of our own psychological states, but rarely do we have that kind of access to their causes (Nisbett & Wilson 1977, Wilson 2002), and this is reason enough to worry that it is going to be quite difficult to separate the influences of conceptual competence from matters of conceptual performance.

The Methodological Conception

It is important to be clear that the problem with the etiological approach is that it is hard to see how it's going to work in practice. The nature of the cognitive processes involved makes it difficult to distinguish conceptual competence from conceptual performance, and their relative inaccessibility, especially to introspection, makes it difficult to see how we are going to be able to determine which mental states count as philosophical intuitions. This has led some philosophers to suggest that there is a *methodological* difference between philosophical intuitions and other kinds of mental states. The idea is that what makes philosophical intuitions different from other kinds of mental states isn't necessarily where they come from but rather what we do with them once they are here. Antti Kauppinen (2007) advocates this approach, arguing that philosophical intuitions are those mental states subjected to critical examination as part of reflective participation in traditional philosophical discourse; they are the mental states ratified by a process of *philosophical reflection*. This way of thinking about things is perfectly consistent with thinking that philosophical intuitions have some kind of special propositional content, special phenomenological characteristic, or even special etiological background. In fact, Kauppinen endorses both an etiological conception and a methodological one, arguing that philosophical intuitions are what competent users of the relevant concepts would say in sufficiently ideal conditions where their judgments are influenced only by semantic considerations, and that these just happen to be the kinds of mental states that are generated by reflective participation in traditional philosophical discourse.

The advantage that the methodological conception has over these other ways of thinking about philosophical intuitions is that it provides a practical way of deciding which mental states count as philosophical intuitions, and does so in a way that seems less likely than the phenomenological or semantic approaches to leave too much out. Still the idea that philosophical intuitions are the product of traditional philosophical reflection does raise some worries about their epistemic fitness, as we will see in later chapters. There are significant, and often overlooked, limits to the epistemic value of traditional kinds of philosophical reflection, a point made nicely by Hilary Kornblith:[15]

When we stop to reflect on the question of whether our pre-reflective beliefs are justified, a host of different biases go to work. We better remember evidence which supports the beliefs we hold than evidence we encountered which runs contrary to them. We better remember occasions on which we have been correct than those on which we have erred. We have a tendency to judge arguments which support our beliefs quite favorably, while arguments which run contrary to our beliefs are held to a very high standard. When we form judgments about the processes by which our pre-reflective beliefs were formed, we seem to employ as a minor premise the belief that we are, all things considered, quite reliable in our judgments, and we thus have a strong tendency to see our beliefs as based on evidence which we ourselves take to be highly probative, whether the beliefs were in fact formed on such a basis or not. As a result, far more often than not, the result of reflection turns out to be little more than a ratification of the beliefs held prior to reflective evaluation. Rather than serving as a source of correction . . . reflection tends to act in ways which further cement our pre-reflective beliefs into place within the larger web of our convictions. Many reflective processes thus act, not to correct our pre-reflective beliefs, but only to increase our confidence in them; we thus become more self-satisfied, even if no more accurate, epistemic agents. (2010, p. 5)

Reflection, it seems, sometimes has quite a negative epistemic influence on us, a point that we will want to look at more closely in coming chapters.

4. Conclusion

Although we haven't settled on an account of philosophical intuitions, hopefully we have a better sense for the different conceptions currently in use in contemporary philosophy, and for their various strengths and weaknesses. While philosophers disagree about the precise nature of philosophical intuitions, there is widespread agreement about the role that they play in contemporary philosophical practice, and hopefully we have a better sense for what that role is supposed to be. We advance philosophical theories on the basis of their ability to explain our philosophical intuitions, and appeal to them as evidence that those theories are true and reasons for believing as such. In the coming chapters, we will see how experimental philosophy emerges from this way of thinking about philosophy, and examine how experimental philosophy might both complement this way of doing philosophy and help identify ways in which it should be reformed.

2

Experimental Philosophy and Philosophical Analysis

1. Introduction

When philosophers want to understand the nature of things like knowledge or moral responsibility, they often construct hypothetical cases designed to draw out our philosophical intuitions about these things. These intuitions play an important role in philosophy, helping philosophers decide which theories to advance and defend, and providing them with a means to do so. This way of thinking about philosophy is most commonly associated with philosophical analysis, which frequently involves arguments that move from people's philosophy intuitions to claims about the truth or plausibility of specific philosophical theories, and some experimental philosophers see themselves as contributing to this philosophical project. They pursue the same philosophical questions as more traditional analytic philosophers, but employ methods that are better suited to the careful study of philosophical intuitions, namely, the methods of the social and cognitive sciences.

In this chapter, we will look at some recent work by experimental philosophers that focuses on the role that philosophical intuitions play in metaphysical discussions about the relationship between freedom and moral responsibility and in epistemological discussions about whether knowledge, or our willingness to attribute knowledge, is influenced by stakes (i.e., the personal cost of being wrong) or salience (i.e., what other possibilities are relevant in a given conversational context). Experimental philosophers have sought to contribute to these discussions through careful empirical investigation of the relevant intuitions and the cognitive processes that shape them. The results have been surprising, revealing interesting things not only about our metaphysical and epistemic intuitions but also about the nature of these metaphysical and epistemological discussions and whether philosophical intuitions are well suited to help move these discussions forward at this time.

2. Experimental Philosophy, Freedom, and Moral Responsibility

Philosophical discussions about the nature of freedom and moral responsibility often begin with the assumption that people are *natural incompatibilists*, believing that neither free will nor moral responsibility is compatible with causal determinism.[1] This purported fact about people is sometimes used as evidence for philosophical theories that contend that free will and moral responsibility actually are incompatible with causal determinism and sometimes used to suggest that philosophical theories that claim otherwise inherit a significant argumentative burden to show that compatibilism is true despite our intuitions to the contrary.

In an influential study of philosophical intuitions about free will and moral responsibility, Eddy Nahmias, Stephen Morris, Thomas Nadelhoffer, and Jason Turner (2004, 2005, 2006) challenged the assumption that people are natural incompatibilists. Consider the following vignette:

Supercomputer:
Imagine that in the next century we discover all the laws of nature, and we build a supercomputer which can deduce from these laws of nature and from the current state of everything in the world exactly what will be happening in the world at any future time. It can look at everything about the way the world is and predict

everything about how it will be with 100% accuracy. Suppose that such a supercomputer existed, and it looks at the state of the universe at a certain time on March 25, 2150 A.D., twenty years before Jeremy Hall is born. The computer then deduces from this information and the laws of nature that Jeremy will definitely rob Fidelity Bank at 6:00 PM on January 26, 2195. As always, the supercomputer's prediction is correct; Jeremy robs Fidelity Bank at 6:00 PM on January 26, 2195.

If people are natural incompatibilists, then we should expect to find that most people asked to consider the *Supercomputer* case would judge that Jeremy did not act of his own free will when he robbed the bank and is not morally responsible for his actions. Somewhat surprisingly, then, Nahmias et al. found just the opposite. They found that most people who are asked to consider the *Supercomputer* case judge that Jeremy acted of his own free will when he robbed the bank and is morally responsible for his actions.[2] This suggests that people might actually be *natural compatibilists*, believing that free will and moral responsibility are in fact compatible with causal determinism. If people are natural compatibilists, then this suggests that it is compatibilism that should be afforded a significant default positive epistemic status and that incompatibilism inherits the argumentative burden of having to show that it is true despite our intuitions to the contrary.

While this would suggest a reversal of fortune in the philosophical discussion about free will and moral responsibility, Shaun Nichols and Joshua Knobe (2007) suggest that we can reconcile these results with the view that people are natural incompatibilists by paying close attention to the role that *affect* is playing in generating the relevant philosophical intuitions. According to Nichols and Knobe, while people are natural incompatibilists, they can come to form compatibilist intuitive judgments when presented with affectively charged vignettes. The underlying idea is that people's emotional responses to the affectively charged vignettes serve to distort their judgments about whether moral responsibility is compatible with causal determinism, drawing them away from their natural incompatibilism to an *unnatural compatibilism*. If this were right, then it would seem that we could explain the fact that most people asked to consider the *Supercomputer* case judge that Jeremy acted of his own free will and is morally responsible for his actions without having to abandon the view that people are natural incompatibilists.

But, is this view right? Are people natural incompatibilists whose intuitive judgments are distorted by their emotional responses to affectively charged vignettes? In order to see whether this is the case, Nichols and Knobe ran a study involving both abstract questions lacking affectively charged content and concrete cases having affectively charged content. Nichols and Knobe began by providing people with the following descriptions of determinism and indeterminism:

> Imagine a universe (Universe A) in which everything that happens is completely caused by whatever happened before it. This is true from the very beginning of the universe, so what happened in the beginning of the universe caused what happened next, and so on right up until the present. For example, one day John decided to have French Fries at lunch. Like everything else, this decision was completely caused by what happened before it. So, if everything in this universe was exactly the same up until John made his decision, then it *had to happen* that John would decide to have French Fries.
>
> Now, imagine a universe (Universe B) in which *almost* everything that happens is completely caused by whatever happened before it. The one exception is human decision making. For example, one day Mary decided to have French Fries at lunch. Since a person's decision in this universe is not completely caused by what happened before it, even if everything in the universe was exactly the same up until Mary made her decision, it *did not have to happen* that Mary would decide to have French Fries. She could have decided to have something different.
>
> The key difference, then, is that in Universe A every decision is completely caused by what happened before the decision – given the past, each decision *has to happen* in the way that it does. By contrast, in Universe B, decisions are not completely caused by the past, and each human decision *does **not** have to happen* the way that it does.[3]

Nichols and Knobe found that after reading the descriptions of determinism and indeterminism, most people who are asked whether it is possible in Universe A for an agent to be morally responsible for her actions judge that it is not possible.[4] That is, most people when asked an abstract question about the compatibility of causal determinism and moral responsibility judge that the two are, in fact, incompatible. But, consider the following vignette:

> *Murderous Husband*:
> In Universe A, a man named Bill has become attracted to his secretary, and he decides that the only way to be with her is to kill his wife and 3 children. He knows that it is impossible to escape from his house in the event of a fire. Before he leaves on a business trip, he sets up a device in his basement that burns down the house and kills his family.

Interestingly, Nichols and Knobe found that most people who were asked to consider the *Murderous Husband* case judge that Bill is morally responsible for killing his wife and children even though his actions were causally determined.[5] It seems, then, that people are natural incompatibilists when presented with abstract questions lacking affectively charged content, but that they come to form compatibilist intuitive judgments when presented with concrete cases possessing affectively charged content.[6] Nichols and Knobe contend that what explains this fact is that people's emotional responses are distorting their judgments. While this doesn't go far enough to show that incompatibilism is true, it does suggest that maybe Nahmias et al. were too quick to conclude that people are *natural* compatibilists. Instead, we might say that people are *unnatural compatibilists*.

There is a problem, however, with attempting to explain away the observed variation as a matter of *performance error*.[7] To describe one process as interfering with another presupposes an understanding of the processes involved. If we already have a well-worked-out account of the particular mechanisms responsible for our *moral responsibility* judgments or a characterization of the function that the cognitive mechanism responsible for these judgments is supposed to compute, then we might be in a position to determine whether or not our emotional responses interfere with the proper function of those mechanisms – that is, whether or not the influence of our emotional responses constitutes a performance error. The problem is that we don't have this. What we have is extensional, distribution data: given scenario x under conditions y, a certain percentage of subjects give answer z. But this provides only an input/output account of what function the mechanism is computing.[8] It doesn't provide us with an understanding of how this computational process is implemented, in particular about the relevant representations and algorithms, or how this computational process is realized physically.[9] Without something like this kind of information, at least in the background, it becomes quite difficult to separate factors that contribute to competence from factors that contribute to performance error, especially when we are dealing with large, systematic variation. So, it seems that Nichols and Knobe simply aren't in a good position to conclude that people are natural incompatibilists who are drawn to some unnatural form of compatibilism by their emotional responses to affectively charged content. In the absence of the right kind of account, which they just don't seem to have, of the particular mechanisms responsible for our *moral responsibility* judgments, we simply cannot tell.

There is another possibility that we've overlooked so far. Maybe *some* people are natural compatibilists, while *others* are natural incompatibilists. For example, maybe there are multiple concepts of *moral responsibility*, according to some of which freedom and moral responsibility are compatible with causal determinism, and according to others of which freedom and moral responsibility are incompatible with causal determinism. This possibility is suggested by the fact that empirical studies demonstrate that hypothetical cases give rise to a number of *different* intuitive responses and is underscored by recent empirical studies that suggest that personality differences can affect whether people are natural compatibilists or natural incompatibilists (see, e.g., Feltz & Cokely 2009). This possibility also has the advantage of bypassing the problem just raised for Nichols and Knobe's unnatural compatibilism view. Since we would no longer be called upon to explain away observed variation in terms of performance errors, our inability to tell whether or not our emotional responses to affectively charged content is part of our competence at making *moral responsibility* judgments loses some of its sting.

In order to see whether or not it is true that some people are natural compatibilists while others are natural incompatibilists, Adam Feltz, Edward Cokely, and Thomas Nadelhoffer (2009) ran a study asking people to consider vignettes containing affectively charged content *and* vignettes lacking affectively charged content.

In particular, they had people consider the following two vignettes, borrowed from Nichols and Knobe (2007):

Serial Rapist:
[In a deterministic universe], as he has done many times in the past, Bill stalks and rapes a stranger.

Habitual Tax Cheat:
[In a deterministic universe], as he has done many times in the past, Mark arranges to cheat on his taxes.

Interestingly, Feltz et al. found that most people who were asked to consider both cases either judged that neither Bill nor Mark is morally responsible for his actions or judged that both Bill and Mark are morally responsible for their actions.[10] These results are consistent with what they call the *multiple concepts view* – the view that some people are natural compatibilists while others are natural incompatibilists. Additionally, these results are inconsistent with the other positions that we've considered. Natural incompatibilism would have predicted that most people would judge that neither Bill nor Mark is morally responsible for his actions, natural compatibilism would have predicted that most people would judge that both Bill and Mark are morally responsible for their actions, and unnatural compatibilism would have predicted that most people would judge that Bill is morally responsible for his actions (because this case is affectively charged) but that Mark is not morally responsible for his actions (because this case is not affectively charged). Since none of these expectations was realized, it seems that we have additional reason to doubt these views.

The multiple concepts view is not without its own problems, however. In particular, it creates a troublesome dilemma.[11] Philosophers are interested in moving from claims about people's shared intuitive judgments to claims about the epistemic standing of philosophical theories. But, if some people are natural compatibilists while others are natural incompatibilists, then we shouldn't expect to find shared intuitive judgments. Two options seem available. On the one hand, philosophers can opt to select one from among the different intuitive judgments that are generated in response to any given real or hypothetical case. But, philosophers taking this option inherit the problem of explaining why the other intuitive judgments should be discounted. And, as the growing literature in the episte- mology of disagreement demonstrates, determining just what to do when confronted with conflicting evidence is not especially straight- forward.[12] On the other hand, philosophers can opt to relativize their conclusions.[13] But, while such a move might be appropriate in some instances, this option is unlikely to prove generally attractive. In particular, it has been historically difficult to move from *descrip- tive* relativism, the view that certain groups of people have different ways of thinking about things, to *normative* relativism, the view that the right way to think about things is relative to certain groups of people. Since one option isn't particularly straightforward and the other isn't particularly attractive, the multiple concepts view poses a significant challenge to the idea that we can move straightforwardly and unproblematically from claims about people's philosophical intuitions about moral responsibility to claims about the truth or plausibility of certain philosophical theories of moral responsibility, one that has yet to be answered.[14]

At this point, it is natural to wonder what progress has been made.[15] Experimental philosophers were initially drawn to philosophical discussions about the nature of free will and moral responsibility because these discussions typically involve appeals to philosophical intuitions. Compatibilists and incompatibilists alike trade on argu- ments that moved from claims about people's intuitive judgments to claims about the truth or plausibility of philosophical theories about the compatibility of freedom, moral responsibility, and causal determinism. Experimental philosophers hoped to help move these discussions forward by providing a clear picture of the relevant intui- tions themselves and insight into the psychological mechanisms and influences that shape them. A clear picture of the relevant intuitions would help us determine which arguments to accept and which to reject. But reality has turned out to be more complicated than expected. Instead of coming to have a single clear picture of the relevant intuitions, we have come to have several competing pic- tures: maybe people are natural compatibilists, believing that free will and moral responsibility are compatible with causal determinism; maybe people are natural incompatibilists who are drawn to some unnatural form of compatibilism by their emotional responses to affectively charged content; maybe there is no single set of intuitions about the compatibility of free will, moral responsibility, and causal determinism. Since we don't yet know which picture is right, we can't determine which arguments to accept and which to reject. We simply can't move the discussion forward at this time. But it is important to see that recognizing this fact, that right now philosophical discussions about the nature of free will and moral responsibility can't progress on the basis of our intuitive judgments about real or hypothetical cases, is itself *progress* and is a significant contribution to the state of play in contemporary philosophical discussions of free will and moral responsibility. After all, sometimes finding out that you can't use a certain tool, at least right now, is just as important as coming to find the right tool to use.

3. Experimental Philosophy and Epistemology

One of the most richly debated questions in contemporary epistemology is whether or not knowledge attributions are sensitive to conversational context. At issue is how to make sense of pairs of vignettes like the following (DeRose 1992):[16]

Bank Case A:
My wife and I are driving home on a Friday afternoon. We plan to stop at the bank on the way home to deposit our paychecks. But as we drive past the bank, we notice that the lines inside are very long, as they often are on Friday afternoons. Although we generally like to deposit our paychecks as soon as possible, it is not especially important in this case that they be deposited right away, so I suggest that we drive straight home and deposit our paychecks on Saturday morning. My wife says, "Maybe the bank won't be open tomorrow. Lots of banks are closed on Saturdays." I reply, "No, I know it'll be open. I was just there two weeks ago on Saturday. It's open until noon."

Bank Case B:
My wife and I drive past the bank on a Friday afternoon, as in Bank Case A, and notice the long lines. I again suggest that we deposit our paychecks on Saturday morning, explaining that I was at the

bank on Saturday morning only two weeks ago and discovered that it was open until noon. But in this case, we have just written a very large and very important check. If our paychecks are not deposited into our checking account before Monday morning, the important check we wrote will bounce, leaving us in a *very* bad situation. And, of course, the bank is not open on Sunday. My wife reminds me of these facts. She then says, "Banks do change their hours. Do you know the bank will be open tomorrow?" Remaining as confident as I was before that the bank will be open then, still, I reply, "Well, no. I'd better go in and make sure."

On one side of the debate, *contextualists* have argued that our intuitive responses to these and similar vignettes show that various features of a conversational context, in particular, what possibilities are made salient, can affect the truth-value of knowledge attributions.[17] On the other side of the debate, *subject-sensitive invariantists* have argued that conversational context does not affect the truth-value of knowledge attributions and that our intuitive responses to these and similar vignettes can best be explained in other ways, for example, in terms of what is at stake for the person whose epistemic position is described.[18]

What has made this debate particularly interesting to experimental philosophers is that both sides of the debate commonly appeal to the very same intuitions about the very same hypothetical cases. What has been at issue is not what the relevant intuitions are, but how best to explain them: do they provide evidence that salience matters or evidence that stakes matter?[19] But this is not the only reason why experimental philosophers have recently become attracted to the debate between contextualists and invariantists. As Jonathan Schaffer (2005) has pointed out, the very same thing that makes this debate particularly interesting has also contributed to its having been particularly intractable: the hypothetical cases commonly employed in the debate tend to differ both in terms of what possibilities are made salient *and* what is at stake. This means that the relevant intuitions just can't tell us what we want to know – that is, they can't tell us what matters. And this provides an additional reason for experimental philosophers to be interested in the debate between contextualists and subject-sensitive invariantists. Experimental philosophers might be able to move the debate forward by carefully studying the right kind of vignettes: vignettes that keep what is at stake separate from what possibilities have been made salient.

Let's start by considering the view that salience matters. According to many contextualists, whether someone knows something (or, at least, counts as knowing something) depends, at least in part, on what possibilities have been made salient. Contextualists rest their case on our purported intuitions about the two bank cases just considered or other cases having similar structure. In both cases, a husband and wife stop by a bank on their way home from work on a Friday afternoon intending to deposit their paychecks. When they notice that the lines inside are quite long, the husband suggests that he come back the following day to make the deposits, noting to his wife that he knows that the bank will be open on Saturday because he was there two Saturdays ago. The only relevant difference between the two cases is supposed to be that in the second case, unlike the first, the wife explicitly raises the possibility that the husband might be wrong, noting that banks sometimes change their hours. Contextualists think that our intuitions will track this difference and, in particular, that we will be more willing to say that the husband knows that the bank is open in *Bank Case A* than we will in *Bank Case B*. This shift in our intuitions is supposed to count as evidence that salience matters and this, in turn, is supposed to count as evidence that contextualism is true.

This argument rests on a testable empirical claim, namely, that our intuitions track what possibilities have been made salient, and a number of experimental studies have recently been conducted in order to test this claim using vignettes designed to ensure that the only difference between vignettes is what possibilities have been made salient. Somewhat surprisingly, the results of some of these studies suggest that salience *doesn't* matter: people seem to be just as willing to say that someone knows something when the possibility of being wrong has been made salient as they are to say that someone knows something when that possibility has gone unmentioned.

Consider, for example, the following pair of vignettes (Buckwalter 2010):

Low Standards
Sylvie and Bruno are driving home from work on a Friday after-noon. They plan to stop at the bank to deposit their paychecks,

but as they drive past the bank they notice that the lines inside are very long. Although they generally like to deposit their paychecks as soon as possible, it is not especially important in this case that they be deposited right away. Bruno tells Sylvie, "I was just here last week and I know that the bank will be open on Saturday." Instead, Bruno suggests that they drive straight home and return to deposit their paychecks on Saturday. When they return to the bank on Saturday, it is open for business.

High Standards

Sylvie and Bruno are driving home from work on Friday afternoon. They plan to stop at the bank to deposit their paychecks, but as they drive past the bank they notice that the lines inside are very long. Although they generally like to deposit their paychecks as soon as possible, it is not especially important in this case that they be deposited right away. Bruno tells Sylvie, "I was just here last week and I know that the bank will be open on Saturday." Instead, Bruno suggests that they drive straight home and return to deposit their paychecks on Saturday. Sylvie says, "Banks are typically closed on Saturday. Maybe this bank won't be open tomorrow either. Banks can always change their hours; I remember this bank used to have different hours." When they return to the bank on Saturday morning, it is open for business.

Unlike *Bank Case A* and *Bank Case B*, the only difference between these two cases is that in the *High Standards* case, unlike the *Low Standards* case, the possibility that Bruno is wrong has been explicitly raised. If contextualists are right, we should expect that people who are asked to consider the *Low Standards* case would be more likely to judge that Bruno knows that the bank will be open on Saturday than people who are asked to consider the *High Standards* case. But, this isn't what happens. Wesley Buckwalter (2010) found no statistically significant difference between intuitive judgments about the two cases: people are just as likely to judge that Bruno knows that the bank will be open on Saturday when they are asked to consider the *High Standards* case as they are when they are asked to consider the *Low Standards* case.[20]

Perhaps salience matters only when stakes matter. Both of Buckwalter's vignettes describe cases in which there is no personal cost associated with being wrong; in both cases, it is not especially important that the paychecks be deposited right away. Maybe the situation would be different were it important that the paychecks be deposited right away. Consider, for example, the following pair of vignettes (May et al. 2010):

High Stakes No Alternative
Hannah and her wife Sarah are driving home on a Friday afternoon. They plan to stop at the bank on the way home to deposit their paychecks. Since they have an impending bill coming due, and very little in their account, it is *very important* that they deposit their paychecks by Saturday. As they drive past the bank, they notice that the lines inside are very long, as they often are on Friday afternoons. Hannah notes that she was at the bank 2 weeks before on a Saturday morning, and it was open. Hannah says, "I know the bank will be open tomorrow. So we can deposit our paychecks tomorrow morning."

High Stakes Alternative
Hannah and her wife Sarah are driving home on a Friday afternoon. They plan to stop at the bank on the way home to deposit their paychecks. Since they have an impending bill coming due, and very little in their account, it is *very important* that they deposit their paychecks by Saturday. As they drive past the bank, they notice that the lines inside are very long, as they often are on Friday afternoons. Hannah notes that she was at the bank 2 weeks before on a Saturday morning, and it was open. *Sarah points out that banks do change their hours.* Hannah says, "I know the bank will be open tomorrow. So we can deposit our paychecks tomorrow morning."

Unlike Buckwalter's two bank cases, the stakes in both of these cases are quite high. If salience matters more when stakes matter, then we should expect that people who are asked to consider the *High Stakes No Alternative* case would be more likely to judge that Hannah knows that the bank will be open on Saturday than people who are asked to consider the *High Stakes Alternative* case. But, again, this expectation is not met. Joshua May, Walter Sinnott-Armstrong, Jay Hull, and Aaron Zimmerman (2010) found no statistically significant difference between intuitive judgments about the two cases.[21]

These studies suggest that contextualists are wrong. In each of the studies just rehearsed, efforts were made to ensure that the only difference between pairs of vignettes concerned whether or not the possibility of being wrong was made salient. Contextualists predict that people's intuitive judgments will track this difference and, yet, people seemed to be just as willing to say that someone knows something when the possibility of being wrong was made salient as they were to say that someone knows something when that possibility went unmentioned. Salience, it seems, *doesn't* really matter.[22]

If salience doesn't matter, then what about stakes? According to subject-sensitive invariantists, whether someone knows something depends, at least in part, on facts about the personal costs associated with being wrong. This marks a significant break from more traditional accounts of knowledge, according to which the only facts relevant to whether or not someone knows something are *truth-conducive* facts, and is part of a growing *anti-intellectualist* trend in recent epistemology.[23] Like contextualists, subject-sensitive invariantists rest their case on our purported intuitions about pairs of vignettes. Consider, for example, the following two vignettes (Stanley 2005):

Low Stakes:
Hannah and her wife Sarah are driving home on a Friday afternoon. They plan to stop at the bank on the way home to deposit their paychecks. It is not important that they do so, as they have no impending bills. But as they drive past the bank, they notice that the lines inside are very long, as they often are on Friday afternoons. Realizing that it isn't very important that their paychecks are deposited right away, Hannah says, "I know the bank will be open tomorrow, since I was there just 2 weeks ago on Saturday morning. So we can deposit our paychecks tomorrow morning."

High Stakes:
Hannah and her wife Sarah are driving home on a Friday afternoon. They plan to stop at the bank on the way home to deposit their paychecks. Since they have an impending bill coming due, and very little in their account, it is very important that they deposit their paychecks by Saturday. Hannah notes that she was at the bank 2 weeks before on Saturday morning, and it was open. But, as Sarah points out, banks do change their hours. Hannah

says, "I guess you're right. I don't know that the bank will be open tomorrow."

Assuming that the bank will be open on Saturday and that the truth-conducive facts available to Hannah don't change from one vignette to the next, then the only relevant difference between the two cases is supposed to be the personal costs associated with being wrong. Since the only relevant differences between the two cases are the personal costs associated with being wrong, and since subject-sensitive invariantists think that our intuitive responses to these vignettes will be that Hannah knows that the bank will be open on Saturday in the *Low Stakes* case but not in the *High Stakes* case, they conclude that stakes matter.

Again, the claim that we will intuitively judge that Hannah knows that the bank will be open on Saturday in the *Low Stakes* case but not in the *High Stakes* case is a testable empirical claim, and experimental philosophers have recently designed a number of studies aimed at testing this claim, making sure that the only difference between pairs of vignettes was the personal costs associated with being wrong. Interestingly, the results of some of these studies suggest that stakes *don't* matter: when truth-conducive facts are fixed across vignettes, people tend to attribute knowledge when the personal costs of being wrong are low *and* when the personal costs of being wrong are high.

Consider, for example, the following pair of vignettes (Feltz & Zarpentine 2010):

Simplified Low Stakes:
Hannah and her sister Sarah are driving home on a Friday afternoon. They plan to stop at the bank on the way home to deposit their paychecks. Since they do not have an impending bill coming due, it is not very important that they deposit their paychecks by Saturday. Hannah notes that she was at the bank two weeks before on a Saturday morning, and it was open. Hannah says to Sarah, "I know that the bank will be open tomorrow."

Simplified High Stakes:
Hannah and her sister Sarah are driving home on a Friday afternoon. They plan to stop at the bank on the way home to deposit their paychecks. Since they have an impending bill coming due,

it is very important that they deposit their paychecks by Saturday. Hannah notes that she was at the bank two weeks before on a Saturday morning, and it was open. Hannah says to Sarah, "I know that the bank will be open tomorrow."

The only difference between the two cases is the personal cost of being wrong. If stakes matter, then we should expect that people who are asked to consider the *Simplified Low Stakes* case would be more likely to judge that Hannah knows that the bank will be open on Saturday than people who are asked to consider the *Simplified High Stakes* case. Interestingly, this doesn't appear to be the case. Adam Feltz and Chris Zarpentine (2010) found no statistically significant difference between intuitive judgments about the two cases.[24]

In a separate empirical study, Mark Phelan (forthcoming) also found that stakes don't seem to matter. Consider the following pair of vignettes:

Unimportant:
Kate is ambling down the street, out on a walk for no particular reason and with no particular place to go. She comes to an intersection and asks a passerby the name of the street. "Main Street," the passerby says. Kate looks at her watch, and it reads 11:45 AM. Kate's eyesight is perfectly normal, and she sees her watch clearly. Kate's hearing is perfectly normal, and she hears the passerby quite well. She has no special reason to believe that the passerby is inaccurate. She also has no special reason to believe that her watch is inaccurate. Kate could gather further evidence that she is on Main Street (she could, for instance, find a map), but she doesn't do so, since, on the basis of what the passerby tells her, she already thinks that she is on Main Street.

Important:
Kate needs to get to Main Street by noon: her life depends on it. She comes to an intersection and asks a passerby the name of the street. "Main Street," the passerby says. Kate looks at her watch, and it reads 11:45 AM. Kate's eyesight is perfectly normal, and she sees her watch clearly. Kate's hearing is perfectly normal, and she hears the passerby quite well. She has no special reason to believe that the passerby is inaccurate. She also has no special

reason to believe that her watch is inaccurate. Kate could gather further evidence that she is on Main Street (she could, for instance, find a map), but she doesn't do so, since, on the basis of what the passerby tells her, she already thinks that she is on Main Street.

As before, the only difference between the two cases is the personal cost of being wrong. So, again, if stakes matter, then we should expect that people who are asked to consider the *Unimportant* case would be more likely to judge that Kate knows that she is on Main Street than people who are asked to consider the *Important* case. But, again, this doesn't appear to be the case. Phelan found no statistically significant difference between intuitive judgments about the two cases.[25]

It looks like stakes don't matter after all. When we put these studies together with the experimental work on salience, the results challenge both contextualism and subject-sensitive invariantism.[26] People seem to be just as willing to say that someone knows something when the possibility of being wrong has been made salient as they are when that possibility has gone unmentioned, and just as willing to say that someone knows something when the personal costs associated with being wrong are high as they are when those costs are low. In light of this, it might be tempting to reject both contextualism and subject-sensitive invariantism in favor of some form of classical invariantism, according to which the truth conditions of knowledge attributions do not vary once the person, proposition, and truth-conducive facts have been settled. There are growing reasons to worry that this move would be too quick, however. Jonathan Schaffer and Joshua Knobe (2011), for example, have recently argued that experimental studies focused on the role that salience plays in knowledge attribution haven't succeeded in making sufficiently salient the possibility that the bank will be closed on Saturday. And, N. Ángel Pinillos (forthcoming) has recently argued that studies focused on the role that stakes play in knowledge attribution haven't made sure that participants are tracking the right details, in particular, the relationship between how much evidence is needed in order to count as knowing something and the personal costs associated with being wrong. Let's look more closely at each of these arguments.

According to Schaffer and Knobe, merely mentioning a possibility does not necessarily make that possibility sufficiently salient, particularly when the possibility mentioned seems strange or improbable.

Instead, the possibility must be presented in a particularly concrete and vivid fashion. This raises a concern about previous experimental studies, namely, that the possibility that the bank will be closed on Saturday wasn't made sufficiently salient in these cases, and that, when that possibility is made sufficiently salient, salience will matter. To test this prediction, Schaffer and Knobe had subjects consider the following pair of vignettes:

Revised Low Standard
Hannah and Sarah are driving home on a Friday afternoon. They plan to stop at the bank to deposit their paychecks. As they drive past the bank, they notice that the lines inside are very long, as they often are on Friday afternoons. Hannah says, "I was at the bank two weeks before on a Saturday morning, and it was open. So this is a bank that is open on Saturdays. We can just leave now and deposit our paychecks tomorrow morning." Sarah replies, "Ok, that sounds good. Let's go on Saturday."

Concrete High Standard
Hannah and Sarah are driving home on a Friday afternoon. They plan to stop at the bank to deposit their paychecks. As they drive past the bank, they notice that the lines inside are very long, as they often are on Friday afternoons. Hannah says, "I was at the bank two weeks before on a Saturday morning, and it was open. So this is a bank that is open on Saturdays. We can just leave now and deposit our paychecks tomorrow morning." Sarah replies, "Well, banks do change their hours sometimes. My brother Leon once got into trouble when the bank changed hours on him and closed on Saturday. How frustrating! Just imagine driving here tomorrow and finding the door locked."

Based on earlier studies that focused on the role that salience plays in knowledge attribution, we should expect no difference: people who are asked to consider the *Concrete High Standard* case should be no less likely to judge that Hannah knows that the bank will be open on Saturday than people who are asked to consider the *Revised Low Standard* case. But, this is not what Schaffer and Knobe found. They found that when the possibility that Hannah is wrong about the bank's weekend hours of operation was raised in this more vivid fashion, people who were asked to consider the *Revised Low Standard* case were, in fact, more likely to judge that Hannah knows that the bank will be open on Saturday than were those people who were asked to consider the *Concrete High Standard* case.[27]

Schaffer and Knobe conclude from this that salience matters after all and go on to use these results (together with other empirical studies) to argue in favor of *contrastivism*, a version of contextualism according to which claims that someone knows something really amount to claims that someone knows something *rather than something else*. But, while these results should certainly give pause to anyone who might have been tempted to reject contextualism on the basis of the results obtained by the Buckwalter (2010) and May et al. (2010) studies, the move by Schaffer and Knobe back to contextualism, or at least to a version of contextualism, also seems too quick. First, since Schaffer and Knobe tested only Australian subjects, this might only be evidence of cross-cultural diversity: maybe salience does matter . . . *for Australians*. (As we shall see in Chapter 4, this isn't an idle concern. The discovery of intuition-based cross-cultural diversity is one of experimental philosophy's most important contributions.) Second, it isn't actually clear that the possibility of being wrong is any more salient in the *Concrete High Standards* case than it is, for example, in the *High Standards* case. In both cases, the protagonist is told that banks sometimes change their hours and this fact is used to underscore the possibility that the particular bank under discussion might not be open on Saturday. In fact, the only significant difference between the two cases seems to be that the protagonist is invited to imagine the personal costs associated with being wrong in the *Concrete High Standards* case. If that is right, then even if we set aside concerns about cross-cultural diversity, it appears that Schaffer and Knobe draw the wrong conclusion. If these cases provide evidence of anything, it seems that they provide evidence that *stakes* matter.

The idea that stakes might matter after all has also received support from recent work by N. Ángel Pinillos (forthcoming). Consider, for example, the following two vignettes (Pinillos, forthcoming):

Low Stakes Typo:
Peter, a good college student, has just finished writing a two-page paper for an English class. The paper is due tomorrow. Even

though Peter is a pretty good speller, he has a dictionary with him that he can use to check and make sure that there are no typos. But very little is at stake. The teacher is just asking for a rough draft and it won't matter if there are a few typos. Nonetheless, Peter would like to have no typos at all.

High Stakes Typo:
John, a good college student, has just finished writing a two-page paper for an English class. The paper is due tomorrow. Even though John is a pretty good speller, he has a dictionary with him that he can use to check and make sure that there are no typos. There is a lot at stake. The teacher is a stickler and guarantees that no one will get an A for the paper if it has a typo. He demands perfection. John, however, finds himself in an unusual circumstance. He needs an A for this paper to get an A in the class. And he needs an A in the class to keep his scholarship. Without the scholarship, he can't stay in school. Leaving college would be devastating for John and his family who have sacrificed a lot to help John through school. So it turns out that it is extremely important for John that there are no typos in this paper. And he is well aware of this.

Pinillos asked people how many times Peter or John would need to proofread the paper before knowing that there are no typos. If stakes don't matter, then we should expect no significant difference in the amount of times people think that John would need to proofread the paper before knowing that there are no typos and the amount of times people think that Peter needs to proofread the paper before knowing that there are no typos. This is *not* what we find; instead, people think that John has to proofread the paper on average 3 more times than Peter in order to know that there are no typos.[28] Putting these results together with the Schaffer and Knobe results, it seems like stakes might matter after all. Still, even these results are contested, with Wesley Buckwalter (forthcoming) arguing that these results indicate less about the relationship between stakes and knowledge attributions than they do about the relationship between stakes and rational action.[29]

What are we to make of the results of all of these studies? On the one hand, we have empirical evidence that suggests that neither stakes nor salience matter. People seem to be just as willing to say that someone knows something when the possibility of being wrong has been made salient as they are when that possibility has gone unmentioned, and people seem just as willing to say that someone knows something when the personal costs associated with being wrong are high as they are when those costs are low. On the other hand, we have empirical evidence that *something* matters – but we aren't able to determine right now whether it's stakes or salience that matter. Complicating things even more, we don't know whether stakes have an epistemic influence on the truth of knowledge attributions or simply practical influence on the rationality of certain kinds of behaviors.[30] We need to be careful drawing conclusions from either set of empirical results at this time.[31] Maybe earlier studies failed to find statistically significant differences because there were no differences to be found; maybe they found no statistically significant differences because the tools they used to test for such differences weren't sufficiently fine-grained or properly tuned. Maybe later studies found a statistically significant difference because the tools that they used to test for such differences were more fine-grained or well tuned than those used in previous studies; maybe later studies found a statistically significant difference because they were studying a different epistemic population. Maybe later studies found that salience matters; maybe later studies found that stakes matter. Maybe stakes matter for knowledge; maybe stakes matter only for rational action. At this point, we just can't tell. Future research is needed. And, this itself has significant implications for philosophers who have used our intuitive judgments about bank cases to advance certain philosophical arguments and positions. Whatever other reasons we might have for adopting some version of contextualism or subject-sensitive invariantism, it seems like more experimental work is going to be needed before our philosophical intuitions can help settle the debate between these two positions.

4. Conclusion

Our philosophical intuitions play a significant role in contemporary discussions of the nature of knowledge and moral responsibility, and experimental philosophers have hoped that empirical work might help move these discussions forward by providing a clear picture of the relevant philosophical intuitions. It turns out that the picture is not so clear. Where we hoped to find consensus, we found conflict. We can accept this, resolve it, or explain it away; but whatever we choose to do, more empirical work is going to be needed. Recognizing this is itself a victory of sorts for experimental philosophy, whose core commitment is that understanding the nature of our philosophical intuitions, and the cognitive processes involved, is something that will require sustained and careful empirical investigation. To see that this investigation is not yet complete is not to see that it isn't needed, but only to see why more is needed.

3

Experimental Philosophy and the Philosophy of Mind

1. Introduction

Philosophers who are interested in *what* philosophical intuitions can tell us owe a story that explains *how* philosophical intuitions can tell us anything at all about ourselves and the world around us. As Alvin Goldman (2007) argues, this story might be particularly hard to tell for philosophers who are interested in what philosophical intuitions might tell us about the non-psychological world.[1] The problem isn't that philosophical intuitions are mental states; so are perceptions and we needn't worry about their ability to tell us things about the non-psychological world. Instead, the problem is that we lack a naturalistically acceptable model of the mechanisms that would connect our philosophical intuitions to the non-psychological world they are supposed to be telling us something about. This kind of worry has motivated some philosophers to turn their attention to what philosophical intuitions can tell us about ourselves. On this view, philosophical intuitions might not be able to tell us what the world is really like, but they can tell us something important about the ways that we think about the world – in particular, about our individual or shared concepts.

In more traditional circles, this interest in what philosophical intuitions can tell us about our individual or shared concepts is associated with *conceptual analysis*. Conceptual analysis aims at identifying the precise meaning of philosophical concepts, and typically involves measuring proposed definitions of philosophical concepts against our philosophical intuitions about the application conditions of those concepts. For example, analytic philosophers might try to identify the precise meaning of *knowledge* by measuring various potential definitions of *knowledge* against our intuitions about when it is, and when it is not, appropriate to attribute knowledge to someone.

The interest in what philosophical intuitions can tell us about ourselves takes a different shape in experimental circles. Many experimental philosophers are less interested in identifying the precise meaning of philosophical concepts than they are in identifying the factors that influence our applications of these concepts. So, for example, experimental philosophers would be less interested in identifying the precise meaning of *knowledge* than they would be in identifying why we have the intuitions that we do about when it is, and when it is not, appropriate to attribute knowledge to someone. The goal is not, or at least not only, to use our intuitions to help explain the meaning of our philosophical concepts, but to explain our intuitions themselves.

In this chapter, we will look at one particularly influential example of this kind of experimental philosophy: namely, recent experimental work on the apparent influence that normative considerations have on people's ordinary ways of thinking about the world. Much of this work has focused on how normative considerations exert this influence, and whether they form part of our *conceptual competence* or simply figure into our *conceptual performance*. It turns out to be quite difficult to determine whether or not normative considerations are part of our conceptual competence, in part because it proves quite difficult to determine precisely how they exert their influence on our ordinary ways of thinking about the world. But, as Hume long ago taught us, even knowing how they do influence our ordinary ways of thinking about the world wouldn't suffice to tell us whether they should have such an influence. And, one of the important lessons from this work is that more (and different) work will be needed before we can determine whether normative considerations are part of our conceptual competence or simply figure into our conceptual performance.

2. The Side-Effect Effect

Sometimes people's intuitions about whether a particular action has been performed intentionally or unintentionally are influenced by *normative* considerations. That is, sometimes when people are evaluating whether or not a given action has been performed intentionally, their judgments are influenced by their beliefs about whether the action (or the outcome of that action) was morally good or morally bad. This seems to be particularly clear when we consider cases involving *foreseen side effects*. (An outcome is a foreseen side effect just in case an agent performs an action that she foresees will bring about the outcome but doesn't perform the action for the purpose of trying to bring it about.) Consider, for example, the following pair of vignettes:

> *Environmental Harm:*
> The vice-president of a company went to the chairman of the board and said, "We are thinking of starting a new program. It will help us increase profits, but it will also harm the environment." The chairman of the board answered, "I don't care at all about harming the environment. I just want to make as much profit as I can. Let's start the new program." They started the new program. Sure enough, the environment was harmed.

> *Environmental Help:*
> The vice-president of a company went to the chairman of the board and said, "We are thinking of starting a new program. It will help us increase profits, and it will also help the environment." The chairman of the board answered, "I don't care at all about helping the environment. I just want to make as much profit as I can. Let's start the new program." They started the new program. Sure enough, the environment was helped.

In one of the most famous findings in experimental philosophy, Joshua Knobe (2003a) found that most people asked to consider the *Environmental Harm* case judge that the chairman intentionally harmed the environment, while most people asked to consider the *Environmental Help* case judge that the chairman did *not* intentionally help the environment.[2] It seems that people are considerably more inclined to judge that an agent brought about a side effect intentionally when they regard that side effect as morally bad than when they regard it as morally good. This provides evidence for the view that people's beliefs about the moral status of an action (or the outcome of that action) influence their intuitions about whether or not the action was performed intentionally.

The apparent influence of moral considerations on people's intentionality judgments is not limited to cases involving side effects. The same influence appears to be found, for example, in cases involving agents who are trying to bring about a certain outcome but lack the skill necessary in order to reliably bring it about. Again, let's consider a pair of vignettes:

No Skill/Positive Outcome:
Jake desperately wants to win the rifle contest. He knows that he will only win the contest if he hits the bull's-eye. He raises the rifle, gets the bull's-eye in the sights, and presses the trigger. But, Jake isn't very good at using his rifle. His hand slips on the barrel of the gun, and the shot goes wild.... Nonetheless, the bullet lands directly on the bull's-eye. Jake wins the contest.

No Skill/Immoral Outcome:
Jake desperately wants to have more money. He knows that he will inherit a lot of money when his aunt dies. One day, he sees his aunt walking by the window. He raises his rifle, gets her in the sights, and presses the trigger. But, Jake isn't very good at using his rifle. His hand slips on the barrel of the gun, and the shot goes wild . . . Nonetheless, the bullet hits her directly in the heart. She dies instantly.

Knobe (2003b) found that most people asked to consider the *No Skill/Immoral Outcome* case judge that Jake intentionally hit his aunt, while most people asked to consider the *No Skill/Positive Outcome* case judge that Jake did *not* intentionally hit the bull's-eye.[3] It seems that people are considerably more inclined to judge that an agent brought about an outcome intentionally when they regard that outcome as morally bad than when they regard it as morally neutral. Again, this provides evidence for the view that people's beliefs about the moral status of an action (or the outcome of that action) influence their intuitions about whether or not the action was performed intentionally.

The studies just examined indicate that people's moral judgments can influence their intuitions about whether or not an action has been performed intentionally. But, what does this mean? Two explanations have dominated the landscape. According to the first explanation, these results tell us something about the relationship between moral judgments and people's use of the word 'intentional' and are best explained in terms of specific features of the underlying mechanisms responsible for our linguistic practices (see, e.g., Adams & Steadman 2004a, 2004b). According to the second explanation, these results tell us something very specific about the relationship between moral judgments and people's concept of *intentional action* and are best explained in terms of specific features of the underlying mechanism responsible for people's judgments about intentional action (see, e.g., Knobe 2003a, 2006, Nadelhoffer 2004a, 2004b, 2006b, Nichols & Ulatowski 2007, and Machery 2008).[4] Let's take each of these explanations in turn.

3. The Side-Effect Effect and Conversational Pragmatics

Fred Adams and Annie Steadman were among the first to attempt to explain the side-effect effect. Adams and Steadman (2004a) suggest that we should be careful about using facts about people's intuitive judgments to reach conclusions about the nature of their underlying concepts. In particular, they argue that the side-effect effect does not tell us anything about the nature of our folk concept of *intentional action* but is, instead, best explained entirely in terms of pragmatic considerations – in particular, in terms of *conversational implicature*.[5] According to Adams and Steadman, people believe that the chairman is blameworthy in the *Environmental Harm* case. This belief introduces a problem. The only way that people can express this belief is by saying that the chairman harmed the environment intentionally. If they said that the chairman did not harm the environment intentionally, then this would imply that the chairman isn't to blame for harming the environment. Recognizing this, when people are asked whether or not the chairman harmed the environment intentionally, they tend to say that he did. This tendency to say that the chairman harmed the environment intentionally doesn't reflect the nature of people's folk concept of *intentional action*, it merely reflects their desire to blame their chairman for harming the environment.[6]

Knobe (2004b) argues that the best way to evaluate the merits of this explanation would be to find a different method for determining whether or not people regard the chairman's actions as intentional – a method that doesn't depend on pragmatic considerations involved in people's use of the word 'intentional'. We could compare the results obtained using this second method against the original results. If the results obtained using the second method differ significantly from the original results, then this would give credence to Adams and Steadman's suggestion that the original results were due to pragmatic considerations and don't tell us anything about the nature of our folk concept of *intentional action*. On the other hand, if the results obtained using the second method agree with the original results, then this would give credence to the suggestion that the original results were *not* due to pragmatic considerations and do tell us something about the nature of our folk concept of *intentional action*.

Knobe (2004b) asked people whether or not the chairman helped or harmed the environment *in order to* increase profits. According to Knobe, people are unwilling to say that someone performed an action in order to achieve a particular goal unless they believe that she performed the action intentionally. As such, asking people whether or not the chairman helped or harmed the environment in order to increase profits provides us with an indirect method of determining whether or not people regard the chairman's action as intentional. Knobe found that most people who were asked to consider the *Environmental Harm* case were willing to say that the chairman harmed the environment in order to increase profits, while most people who were asked to consider the *Environmental Help* case were *not* willing to say that the chairman helped the environment in order to increase profits.[7] Since the results obtained using this second method agreed with the original results, Knobe concluded that the original results were *not* due to pragmatic considerations and did tell us something about the nature of our folk concept of *intentional action*.

Knobe's (2004b) study did little to convince Adams and Steadman.

In a paper responding to this study, Adams and Steadman (2004b) argue that the same pragmatic considerations that played a role in people's willingness to say that the chairman harmed the environment intentionally are playing a role in people's willingness to say that the chairman harmed the environment in order to increase profits. They agree with Knobe that people are unwilling to say that someone performed an action in order to achieve a particular goal unless they believe that she performed the action intentionally. But, they argue, this is precisely why we should suspect that whatever pragmatic considerations played a role in people's willingness to say that the chairman harmed the environment intentionally are playing a role in people's willingness to say that the chairman harmed the environment in order to increase profits.

Adams and Steadman are right. If pragmatic considerations are playing a role in people's willingness to say that the chairman harmed the environment intentionally, then they are also likely playing a role in people's willingness to say that the chairman harmed the environment in order to increase profits. It is not clear, however, that pragmatic considerations are actually playing the role that Adams and Steadman suggest. Malle (2006) points out that people who were asked to consider the *No Skill/Immoral Outcome* case were invited to express blame directly. It is odd to think that people would feel the need to conversationally imply something that they were allowed to express directly.[8] Still, it might be the case that people's attributions of intentionality are influenced by their attributions of blame in a different way: people's attributions of intentionality aren't made in order to conversationally imply blame but are made for the sake of consistency. That is, maybe people feel that it would be inconsistent to say both that someone is to blame for her actions and that she committed those actions unintentionally. But, this also doesn't seem to be the case. Instead, it seems as if people are quite willing to blame others for unintentional actions. Consider the following vignette:

Drunk Driver:
Bob got rip-roaring drunk at a party after work. When the party ended, he stumbled to his car and started driving home. He was very drunk at the time – so drunk that he eventually lost control of his car, swerved into oncoming traffic, and killed a family of five.[9]

Knobe (2003b) found that most people asked to consider this vignette judge that Bob was to blame for killing the family of five even though they also judge that Bob did so unintentionally. So, it seems that people's attributions of intentionality are neither made in order to conversationally imply blame (since the same attributions are made in contexts in which it is possible to directly attribute blame), nor made for sake of consistency (since there are contexts in which people are willing to attribute blame without attributing intentionality). Putting these two considerations together, it seems hard to sustain the suggestion that the side-effect effect is best explained in terms of pragmatic considerations.

4. The Side-Effect Effect and Our Concept of *Intentional Action*

If pragmatic considerations don't adequately explain the side-effect effect, Knobe (2003a, 2006) argues that maybe the effect is telling us something very specific about the relationship between normative judgments and people's concept of *intentional action* and about the proper function of the underlying mechanism responsible for people's judgments about intentional action. This view is actually quite radical, signaling a shift away from the traditional view of our concept of *intentional action* according to which its function is restricted to explaining and predicting behavior. According to Knobe, our concept of *intentional action* plays a role not only in our explanatory and predictive practices, but also in our *evaluative* practices. This allows us to explain the results without having to explain them away. Since our concept of *intentional action* plays a role in our evaluative practices, it is perfectly appropriate for normative judgments to influence intentionality judgments.

Thomas Nadelhoffer (2004a, 2004b, 2006b) agrees with Knobe that these results tell us something about the relationship between people's moral judgments and their concept of *intentional action*. However, he denies that these results tell us something about the proper function of the underlying mechanism responsible for people's judgments about intentional action, arguing instead that they reveal ways in which this mechanism might *malfunction*.[10] Taking

Knobe's *Environmental Harm* case as our model, the general idea is this: people who are asked to consider the *Environmental Harm* case have a negative affective response to the chairman; this negative affective response distorts people's intentionality judgments, causing them to incorrectly judge that the chairman harmed the environment intentionally.[11]

Claiming that people's negative affective judgments are distorting their intentionality judgments, of course, suggests that moral considerations *shouldn't* affect our intentionality judgments. Why not? The reason, according to Nadelhoffer, is that whether or not someone committed an action intentionally is supposed to play a role in determining whether or not she deserves to be held legally responsible for the action. If people's negative affective responses influence their intentionality judgments, and intentionality judgments determine judgments about legal responsibility, then people will be more likely to hold someone legally responsible for her actions when those actions generate strong negative affective responses. To see the problems this might create, consider the following two vignettes:

Police Officer:
Imagine that a thief is driving a car full of recently stolen goods. While he is waiting at a red light, a police officer comes up to the window of the car while brandishing a gun. When he sees the officer, the thief speeds off through the intersection. Amazingly, the officer manages to hold on to the side of the car as it speeds off. The thief swerves in a zigzag fashion in the hope of escaping – knowing full well that doing so places the officer in grave danger. But the thief doesn't care; he just wants to get away. Unfortunately for the officer, the thief's attempt to shake him off is successful. As a result, the officer rolls into oncoming traffic and sustains fatal injuries. He dies minutes later.

Car Thief:
Imagine that a man is waiting in his car at a red light. Suddenly, a car thief approaches his window while brandishing a gun. When he sees the thief, the driver panics and speeds off through the intersection. Amazingly, the thief manages to hold on to the side of the car as it speeds off. The driver swerves in a zigzag fashion in the hope of escaping – knowing full well that doing so places the

thief in grave danger. But the driver doesn't care; he just wants to get away. Unfortunately for the thief, the driver's attempt to shake him off is successful. As a result, the thief rolls into oncoming traffic and sustains fatal injuries. He dies minutes later.

Although the two vignettes are structurally identical, Nadelhoffer (2006b) found that people who are asked to consider the *Police Officer* case form a stronger negative affective response towards the driver of the car than people who are asked to consider the *Car Thief* case.[12] Additionally, people who are asked to consider the *Police Officer* case are more likely to judge that the driver caused the death intentionally than people who are asked to consider the *Car Thief* case.[13] This means that people are more likely to hold the driver legally responsible for the death of the police officer than the death of the car thief. But, according to Nadelhoffer, we don't want the fact that someone is charged with a crime that generates strong negative affective responses to make it more likely that people will find her legally responsible for the crime in question. As such, Nadelhoffer urges that moral considerations *shouldn't* affect our intentionality judgments. The influence of moral considerations on our intentionality judgments signals a malfunction of the underlying mechanism responsible for our judgments about intentional action.

Let's look more closely at this suggestion. The central idea is that people's affective responses are driving (in this case, somewhat recklessly) their intentionality judgments. People feel that the chairman deserves blame for harming the environment and this negative affective response causes them to (incorrectly) judge that he did so intentionally. The problem is that intentionality judgments aren't always emotional. In fact, we find that even people (for example, patients with ventromedial prefrontal cortex damage) who lack the ability to have *any* affective response to the chairman's actions nevertheless judge that the chairman harmed the environment intentionally (Young et al. 2006). This calls into question the suggestion that it is an emotional response to the chairman's actions that is causing people to judge that he harmed the environmental intentionally. Of course, blame isn't always emotional either. It is certainly possible for people to think that the chairman deserves blame for harming the environment without having a corresponding emotional response to the chairman's actions. But, even blame and intentionality come apart, as the *Drunk Driver* case nicely illustrates. People seem perfectly willing to assign blame in cases where an action is thought to be unintentional.[14] Moreover, even in cases where blame and intentionality don't come apart, we find that people generally make intentionality judgments *before* they make judgments of blame (Guglielmo & Malle 2009). This makes it hard to sustain the idea that people judge that the chairman harmed the environment intentionally *because* they want to blame the chairman for doing so.[15] Whatever is driving people's intentionality judgments, it seems that neither *affect* nor *blame* is at the wheel.[16]

Joshua Knobe and Thomas Nadelhoffer agree that these results tell us something about the relationship between people's moral judgments and their concept of *intentional action*. Knobe argues these results tell us something about the proper function of the underlying mechanism responsible for people's judgments about intentional action, while Nadelhoffer argues that these results tell us something about how this mechanism might malfunction. Edouard Machery (2008) challenges both of these views. First, Machery claims that we should remain neutral about whether or not the side-effect effect is best explained in terms of competent intentionality judgments. Second, he claims that the results actually tell us something, not about the relationship between people's moral judgments and their concept of *intentional action*, but about the relationship between people's concept of *intentional action* and considerations of costs and benefits.

Before turning our attention to the second claim, which has garnered the most attention, it is worth spending a few moments looking at Machery's call for neutrality. As we've seen, at least part of what is at issue between Knobe and Nadelhoffer is whether the side-effect effect tells us something about people's *conceptual competence* or about people's *conceptual performance*. The competence/performance distinction traces back to Noam Chomsky's (1965) distinction between linguistic competence and linguistic performance, and has been used to distinguish between a person's knowledge of a given concept and her use of that concept. The central idea is that certain factors (e.g., resource limitations or interference from other cognitive processes) can influence a person's use of a given concept without influencing her knowledge of that concept or being reflective of the meaning of that concept. Knobe thinks that the side-effect

effect tells us something about people's conceptual competence, while Nadelhoffer thinks that it tells us something about people's conceptual performance. The problem is that any resolution of this disagreement would require something that we don't currently have, namely some agreed-upon way of distinguishing what is and what is not constitutive of our folk concept of *intentional action*.[17] Knobe seems willing to let empirical evidence do the work, but the problem with this way of approaching questions of conceptual competence is that the kind of empirical evidence Knobe has in mind isn't particularly well suited to answering these kinds of questions. In order to separate competence from performance, at least in a way that would help resolve this particular debate, we need some sort of account of the kind of work our folk concept of *intentional action* is supposed to be doing for us, and empirical evidence alone simply won't help produce such an account.

Nadelhoffer avoids this problem by simply stipulating what kind of work our folk concept of *intentional action* is supposed to be doing for us. This allows him to maintain that the side-effect effect tells us something about people's conceptual performance, but does so in a way that leaves open the possibility that someone else (Knobe, for example) might simply stipulate a different account according to which the side-effect effect tells us something about people's conceptual competence. Stipulations, after all, are free moves. Of course, there might be other ways of trying to identify what kind of work our folk concept of *intentional action* is supposed to be doing, for example evolutionary or teleological approaches. There might also be ways of grounding the competence/performance distinction that don't require starting with a conception of the kind of work that our folk concept of *intentional action* is supposed to be doing. But, in the absence of either of these things, it seems that the most reasonable thing to do is to remain neutral about whether the side-effect effect is telling us something about people's conceptual competence or their conceptual performance.

With that discussion out of the way, let's look more closely at Machery's second claim, namely that the results actually tell us something, not about the relationship between people's moral judgments and their concept of *intentional action*, but about the relationship between people's concept of *intentional action* and considerations of costs and benefits. Recall that Knobe (2003a) found that most people asked to consider the *Environmental Harm* case judge that the chairman intentionally harmed the environment, while most people asked to consider the *Environmental Help* case judge that the chairman did *not* intentionally help the environment. To explain these results, Machery proposes what he calls the *trade-off hypothesis*. There is a cost associated with increasing profits in the *Environmental Harm* case, namely harming the environment. Since people believe that costs are incurred intentionally, this explains why people asked to consider the *Environmental Harm* case judge that the chairman intentionally harmed the environment. By contrast, there are no costs associated with increasing profits in the *Environmental Help* case. This explains why people asked to consider the *Environmental Help* case judge that the chairman did *not* intentionally help the environment.

Machery supports the trade-off hypothesis with two pairs of vignettes. Let's begin with the first pair:

Extra Dollar:
Joe was feeling quite dehydrated, so he stopped by the local smoothie shop to buy the largest sized drink available. Before ordering, the cashier told him that the Mega-Sized Smoothies were now one dollar more than they used to be. Joe replied, "I don't care if I have to pay one dollar more, I just want the biggest smoothie you have." Sure enough, Joe received the Mega-Sized Smoothie and paid one dollar more for it.[18]

Free Cup:
Joe was feeling quite dehydrated, so he stopped by the local smoothie shop to buy the largest sized drink available. Before ordering, the cashier told him that if he bought a Mega-Sized Smoothie he would get it in a special commemorative cup. Joe replied, "I don't care about a commemorative cup, I just want the biggest smoothie you have." Sure enough, Joe received the Mega-Sized Smoothie in a commemorative cup.

Machery found that most people asked to consider the *Extra Dollar* case judge that Joe intentionally paid an extra dollar, while most people asked to consider the *Free Cup* case judge that Joe did *not* intentionally buy the commemorative cup.[19] Since most people viewed the actions (paying an extra dollar and buy a commemorative cup) as morally neutral, this provides evidence that something other than people's beliefs about the moral status of an action (or the outcome of that action) influence their intuitions about whether or not the action was performed intentionally. Instead, this is evidence that people's intuitions about whether or not an action was performed intentionally are being influenced by simple considerations of costs and benefits.

The apparent influence of simple considerations of costs and benefits on people's intentionality judgments is not limited to cases involving morally neutral actions. The same influence appears to be found, for example, in cases involving morally *appropriate* actions. To see this, let's consider Machery's second pair of vignettes:

Worker:
John is standing near the tracks of a trolley. John notices that the brakes of the trolley have failed. Five workmen are working on the tracks with their backs turned. John sees that the runaway trolley is headed for the five workmen who will be killed if it proceeds on its present course. The only way to save these five workmen is to hit a switch that will turn the trolley onto the side tracks. Unfortunately, there is a single workman on the side tracks with his back turned. John knows that the workman on the side tracks will be killed if he hits the switch, but the five workmen will be saved. John decides to hit the switch. Sure enough, the trolley turns on the sidetracks, the five workmen on the main tracks are saved, and the workman on the side tracks is killed.

Dog:
John is standing near the tracks of a trolley. John notices that the brakes of the trolley have failed. Five workmen are working on the tracks with their backs turned. John sees that the runaway trolley is headed for the five workmen who will be killed if it proceeds on its present course. The only way to save these five workmen is to hit a switch that will turn the trolley onto the side tracks. Moreover, there is a dog on the tracks with its back turned. John knows that the five workmen and the dog will be saved if he hits the switch. John thinks "I don't care at all about saving the dog. I just want to save the five workmen." John decides to hit the

switch. Sure enough, the trolley turns on the side tracks, the five workmen and the dog on the main tracks are saved.

Machery found that most people asked to consider the *Worker* case judge that John intentionally caused the death of the workman on the side tracks, while most people asked to consider the *Dog* case judge that John did *not* intentionally save the dog.[20] Since most people viewed the actions (causing the death of the workman on the side tracks and saving the dog) as morally appropriate actions, this provides additional evidence that something other than people's beliefs about the moral status of an action (or the outcome of that action) influence their intuitions about whether or not the action was performed intentionally.[21] Again, it appears that people's intuitions about whether or not an action was performed intentionally are being influenced by simple considerations of costs and benefits.

Let's look more closely at Machery's trade-off hypothesis, according to which people's intuitions about whether or not an action was performed intentionally are being influenced by simple considerations of costs and benefits. There are two possible readings of this hypothesis.[22] On one reading of the hypothesis, people's intuitions about whether or not an action was performed intentionally are being influenced by the fictional agent's perception of something as a cost. Let's call this reading, the *agent-oriented reading*. On a second reading of the hypothesis, people's intuitions about whether or not an action was performed intentionally are being influenced by their own perceptions of something as a cost. Let's call this reading, the *subject-oriented* reading.

The trouble is that there seem to be significant problems for the trade-off hypothesis on either reading. Let's start with the agent-oriented reading. Ronald Mallon (2009) points out that if people's intuitions about whether or not an action was performed intentionally are being influenced by the fictional agent's perception of something as a cost, then we should expect the side-effect effect to disappear in cases where the fictional agents don't view the relevant side effects as costs. But consider the following two vignettes:

Harmful Terrorist:
A member of a terrorist cell went to the leader and said, "We are thinking of bombing a nightclub. It will kill many Americans,

but it will also harm the Australians since many Australians will be killed too." The leader answered, "I admit that it would be good to harm the Australians, but I don't really care about that. I just want to kill as many Americans as possible! Let's bomb the nightclub!" They did bomb the nightclub, and sure enough, the Australians were harmed since many Australians were killed.

Helpful Terrorist:
A member of a terrorist cell went to the leader and said, "We are thinking of bombing a nightclub. It will kill many Americans, but it will also drive down property costs, helping the nearby orphanage acquire the land it needs for the children." The leader answered, "I admit that it would be good to help the orphanage, but I don't really care about that. I just want to kill as many Americans as possible! Let's bomb the nightclub!" They did bomb the nightclub, and sure enough, the orphanage was helped by falling property values.

Mallon (2009) found that most people asked to consider the *Harmful Terrorist* case judge that the terrorist intentionally harmed the Australians, while most people asked to consider the *Helpful Terrorist* case judge that the terrorist did *not* intentionally help the orphanage.[23] This provides evidence *against* the view that people's intuitions about whether or not an action was performed intentionally are being influenced by the fictional agent's perception of something as a cost. Something else must be influencing people's intuitions about whether or not the action was performed intentionally.

Maybe the subject-oriented reading is right. Mark Phelan and Hagop Sarkissian (2009) point out that if people's intuitions about whether or not an action was performed intentionally are being influenced by their own perception of something as a cost, then we should expect that most people are willing to judge that an action is intentional when they view it as a cost to be incurred in the pursuit of some important goal. But consider the following vignette:

Caring Lieutenant:
A lieutenant was talking with a sergeant. The lieutenant gave the order: "Send your squad to the top of Thompson Hill." The sergeant said: "But if I send my squad to the top of Thompson Hill,

we'll be moving the men directly into the enemy's line of fire. Some of them will surely be killed!" The lieutenant answered: "Look, I know that they'll be in the line of fire, and I know that some of them will be killed. I care about my soldiers more than anyone else. But it's imperative to the success of this campaign that we take Thompson Hill." The squad was sent to the top of Thompson Hill. As expected, the soldiers were moved into the enemy's line of fire, and some of them were killed.

Phelan and Sarkissian found that most people asked to consider the *Caring Lieutenant* case judge that the lieutenant did *not* intentionally cause the soldiers' deaths. Since people generally perceive the soldiers' deaths as a cost, this provides evidence *against* the view that people's intuitions about whether or not an action was performed intentionally are being influenced by their own perceptions of something as a cost.[24,25] Again, something else must be influencing people's intuitions about whether not the action was performed intentionally.

So far we've been considering explanations of the side-effect effect according to which these results tell us something specific about the relationship between normative judgments and people's concept of *intentional action*. All of these explanations assume that there is a single folk concept of *intentional action*. Shaun Nichols and Joseph Ulatowski (2007) challenge this assumption, arguing both that there are multiple folk concepts of *intentional action* and that the side-effect effect is better explained as telling us something about the relationship between normative judgments and these different folk concepts of *intentional action*.

At issue is how best to explain minority responses. While most people asked to consider the *Environmental Harm* case judge that the chairman intentionally harmed the environment and most people asked to consider the *Environmental Help* case judge that the chairman did not intentionally help the environment, responses aren't univocal. Some people asked to consider the *Environmental Harm* case judge that the chairman did not intentionally harm the environment and some people asked to consider the *Environmental Help* case judge that the chairman intentionally helped the environment. How should we explain these minority responses?

Typically, such responses are treated as noise resulting from some kind of performance error. Nichols and Ulatowski (2007) suggest a different explanation. They asked people to consider *both* the *Environmental Harm* case and the *Environmental Help* case. They found an interesting pattern of responses. Some people asked to consider both cases provide asymmetric responses, judging that the chairman intentionally harmed the environment but did not intentionally help the environment. Other people asked to consider both cases provide symmetric responses, judging either that the chairman both intentionally harmed the environment and intentionally helped the environment or that the chairman neither intentionally harmed the environment nor intentionally helped the environment. Additionally, they found that people who judge that the chairman intentionally harmed the environment typically explain their judgments by appealing to the chairman's *belief* that the environment would be harmed and that people who judge that the chairman did not intentionally help the environment typically explain their judgments by appealing to the chairman's lacking the *desire* to help the environment. This pattern of responses, and corresponding set of explanations, leads Nichols and Ulatowski to suggest that there are actually two separate folk concepts of *intentional action*, one involving an epistemic component and the other involving a motivational component.

Fiery Cushman and Alfred Mele (2008) point out a problem with Nichols and Ulatowski's view that there are two distinct concepts of *intentional action*, one involving an epistemic component and the other involving a motivational component. In both the *Environmental Harm* case and the *Environmental Help* case, the chairman has a belief about what impact the profit-making venture will have on the environment but lacks the relevant desire to either harm or help the environment. Cushman and Mele wonder how people would respond to cases in which the agent has the relevant desire but lacks the relevant belief. Cushman and Mele predict that, if Nichols and Ulatowski are right, three things should happen. First, people working with the epistemic concept should be more likely to judge that an agent has acted intentionally when she has the relevant belief but lacks the relevant desire than when she has the relevant desire but lacks the relevant belief. Second, people working with the motivational concept should be more likely to judge that an agent has acted intentionally when she has the relevant desire but lacks the relevant belief than when she has the relevant belief but lacks the relevant desire. Third, people working with the motivational concept should be more likely than people working with the epistemic concept to judge that an agent has acted intentionally when she has the relevant desire but lacks the relevant belief. Contrary to two of these predictions, Cushman and Mele found that people working with the motivational concept were not more likely than people working with the epistemic concept to judge that an agent has acted intentionally when she has the relevant desire but lacks the relevant belief, and that people working with the epistemic concept were not more likely to judge that an agent has acted intentionally when she has the relevant belief but lacks the relevant desire than when she has the relevant desire but lacks the relevant belief. Cushman and Mele conclude that there are actually more than two distinct concepts of *intentional action*: one that treats desire as a necessary condition for intentional action; another that treats it as a sufficient condition for intentional action; and yet another that treats it as a sufficient condition for intentional action *only in cases of morally bad actions*.

However many concepts are involved, the advantage of a multiple concept explanation is that it explains minority responses without having to explain them away. It also provides a neat explanation of the side-effect effect itself. In the *Environmental Harm* case, the chairman knowingly harms the environment but does not care at all about harming it; in the *Environmental Help* case, the chairman knowingly helps the environment but does not care at all about helping it. What explains the fact that most people asked to consider the *Environmental Harm* case judge that the chairman intentionally harmed the environment, while most people asked to consider the *Environmental Help* case judge that the chairman did not intentionally help the environment is that different normative judgments trigger different concepts of *intentional action*.

5. Conclusion

It seems that the side-effect effect is telling us *something* about the relationship between normative considerations and our concept – or concepts – of *intentional action*. Dean Pettit and Joshua Knobe (2009) suggest that the sphere of influence is even wider, arguing that it tells us something about the relationship between normative considerations and folk psychology *in general*. They found that normative considerations influence a wide variety of folk psychological judgments, including judgments about decision, desire, preference, advocacy, and choice. Other researchers have recently added studies that suggest that normative considerations influence folk psychological judgments about causation (Hitchcock & Knobe 2009, Roxborough & Cumby 2009) and knowledge (Beebe & Buckwalter 2010). With more studies emerging all of the time, it now seems like we are only beginning to comprehend just how widespread this influence may be.

It also remains to be seen just what the side-effect effect is actually telling us. In particular, it remains to be seen whether it is telling us something about our conceptual competence or our conceptual performance. And, here, experimental philosophers face a problem. Determining whether or not the side-effect effect is telling us something about our conceptual competence requires experimental and theoretical resources that experimental philosophers don't currently have. What is needed is some account of the kind of work our folk concepts are supposed to be doing and/or an account of the physical implementation of the relevant cognitive processes and mechanisms. Unfortunately, the kind of experimental methods typically employed by experimental philosophers, namely survey methods, aren't apt to produce either kind of account. What is needed instead, for example, are neuroanatomical accounts of the cognitive processes and mechanisms responsible for our folk psychological judgments and evolutionary (or other teleological) accounts of the work that our folk concepts are supposed to be doing. Developing these kinds of accounts is going to require experimental philosophers to become even *more* experimental by expanding the variety of experimental methods that they employ.

4

Experimental Philosophy and Philosophical Methodology

1. Introduction

The idea that our philosophical intuitions provide us with important philosophical insight about the world and ourselves has not been without its critics, and much of the concern has centered on the purported evidentiary status of philosophical intuitions in debates about the truth or plausibility of philosophical theories. Some have argued that, while philosophical intuitions count as evidence for something, they don't count as evidence for anything that ought to be of real interest to philosophers (see, e.g., Kornblith 1998, 2002, 2007). Others have argued that philosophical intuitions cannot be treated as evidence because we cannot determine antecedently whether or not they are reliable guides to the truth (see, e.g., Cummins 1998). Still others have argued that philosophical intuitions cannot be treated as evidence because they are fallible (e.g., Devitt 1994, Elgin 1996). These challenges have been instructive, but more for what they tell us about what a successful challenge must look like than for what they tell us about the standing of philosophy's interest in our philosophical intuitions. We learn from them that a successful challenge can't rest on too narrow a conception of philosophy, can't demand the epistemically impossible, and can't be so strong that it deems *all* putative evidence untrustworthy.

In this chapter we will focus on a different kind of challenge, one advanced by experimental philosophers, and ask how well it has learned these lessons. Philosophers have been interested in pursuing philosophical questions through the lens of our philosophical intuitions, at least in part, because they've believed that these intuitions are more or less universally shared. Recent empirical work, however, finds interesting patterns of intuitional diversity. While intuitional diversity presents its own methodological challenges, forcing us to either explain away certain evidence or explain away our worries about evidential diversity, the real problem is that these patterns of intuitional diversity suggest that our philosophical intuitions might be sensitive to things that we neither expected nor perhaps wanted them to be. Since unwanted evidential sensitivity is acceptable only when it can be expected and controlled, it seems that philosophy's intuition deploying practices face a challenge.

The exact nature of this challenge, often called the *restrictionist challenge*, and what general methodological conclusions should be drawn from this work, has proven difficult to determine. The most radical version of this challenge would call for a complete methodological elimination of philosophical intuitions, but this position seems too radical, being neither warranted by the empirical results nor necessary in order to accommodate them. The most conservative version of this challenge would call for limited methodological restrictions, removing problematically sensitive philosophical intuitions from play, while leaving our intuition deploying practices otherwise intact. This position seems too conservative, failing to appreciate the risks involved in not knowing how widespread this kind of problematic intuitional sensitivity might be. The right position falls somewhere in between, combining *local* methodological restrictions with a *global* shift in how we think about and approach our intuition deploying practices. The real challenge lies not just in the fact that intuitions are not wholly reliable, but also in the fact that we know so little about them. We lack the resources needed to explain problematic intuitional sensitivity and, in return, struggle to understand its dimensions, to identify strategies for how to compensate for it, and to predict where it will appear. What is really needed, then, is a general, systematic understanding of philosophical intuitions. By coming to better understand what intuitions are, where they come from, and what factors influence them, we can better understand what role they can play in philosophical practice.

2. Intuitional Diversity

We tend to believe that our philosophical intuitions are more or less universally shared. This is what seems at least partially to underwrite our intuition deploying practices. We think of these practices as more than mere intellectual autobiography, and appeal to philosophical intuitions, when we do, because we anticipate that others share our intuitive judgments. But, recent empirical work suggests that we might be wrong: instead of universality, we find diversity.

One of the most widely discussed kinds of intuitional diversity has been *cultural* diversity: our philosophical intuitions seem to be sensitive to our own cultural background.[1] Stephen Stich (1988, 1990) was the first to seriously put forward the idea that cultural background might play a role in shaping our philosophical intuitions. But it wasn't until he teamed up with Jonathan Weinberg and Shaun Nichols (Weinberg et al. 2001, Nichols et al. 2003) in a series of cross-cultural studies on our epistemic intuitions that this idea really began to take root. These cross-cultural studies revealed that, in fact, people from different cultural backgrounds have significantly different epistemic intuitions. Consider the following vignette:

> *American Car*
> Bob has a friend Jill, who has driven a Buick for many years. Bob therefore thinks that Jill drives an American car. He is not aware, however, that her Buick has recently been stolen, and he is also not aware that Jill has replaced it with a Pontiac, which is a different kind of American car. Does Bob really know that Jill drives an American car, or does he only believe it?

If cultural background plays no role in shaping our philosophical intuitions, then we should expect people from different cultural backgrounds to form similar intuitive judgments about this case. Remarkably, this is not what we find. Instead, we find that, while most people from Western backgrounds judge that Bob only believes that Jill drives an American car, most people from East Asian or South Asian backgrounds judge that Bob actually knows that she does.[2] It seems that our intuitions about this case are tracking more than we might have anticipated, and that cultural background is playing *some* role in generating them.

Although we don't know precisely *what* role cultural background is playing in generating philosophical intuitions about this case, we do know that this case is not unique. Not only is cultural diversity not limited to our epistemic intuitions about this particular hypothetical case, it's not limited to epistemic intuitions at all. Recent work in experimental philosophy suggests that some of our semantic intuitions are also culturally diverse (Machery et al. 2004, Mallon et al. 2009). Consider, for example, the following two versions of Kripke's famous *Gödel* case:

Gödel

Suppose that John has learned in college that Gödel is the man who proved an important mathematical theorem, called the incompleteness of arithmetic. John is quite good at mathematics and he can give an accurate statement of the incompleteness theorem, which he attributes to Gödel as the discoverer. But this is the only thing that he has heard about Gödel. Now suppose that Gödel was not the author of this theorem. A man called "Schmidt" whose body was found in Vienna under mysterious circumstances many years ago, actually did the work in question. His friend Gödel somehow got a hold of the manuscript and claimed credit for the work, which was thereafter attributed to Gödel. Thus he has been known as the man who proved the incompleteness of arithmetic. Most people who have heard the name "Gödel" are like John; the claim that Gödel discovered the incompleteness theorem is the only thing that they have ever heard about Gödel.

Tsu Ch'ung Chih

Ivy is a high school student in Hong Kong. In her astronomy class she was taught that Tsu Ch'ung Chih was the man who first determined the precise time of the summer and winter solstices. But, like all her classmates, this is the only thing she has heard about Tsu Ch'ung Chih. Now suppose that Tsu Ch'ung Chih did not really make this discovery. He stole it from an astronomer who died soon after making the discovery. But the theft remained entirely undetected and Tsu Ch'ung Chih became famous for the discovery of the precise times of the solstices. Many people are like Ivy; the claim that Tsu Ch'ung Chih determined the solstice times is the only thing they have ever heard about him.

Remember that our semantic intuitions about cases like these are supposed to help us decide between descriptivist and causal-historical theories of reference. Interestingly, we find that people from East Asian backgrounds are more likely to be descriptivists (believing, for example, that John is referring to Schmidt) than are people from Western backgrounds.[3] This suggests that, while most analytic philosophers followed Kripke's lead by adopting some kind of causal-historical account of reference, this move might be rather unique to Western culture.[4]

It seems that Stich was right: cultural background plays a role in shaping at least some of our philosophical intuitions. But, the story doesn't stop here. Not all intuitional diversity is cultural diversity, and recently focus has shifted to another kind of interpersonal intuitional diversity, namely *gender* diversity (Zamzow & Nichols 2009, Stich & Buckwalter 2011, Buckwalter & Stich, forthcoming). Consider the following two versions of the famous *Trolley* case:

Stranger
You are taking your daily walk near the train tracks and you notice that the train that is approaching is out of control. You see what has happened: the driver of the train saw five people working on the tracks and slammed on the brakes, but the brakes failed and the driver fainted. The train is now rushing toward the five people. It is moving so fast that they will not be able to get off the track in time. You happen to be standing next to a switch, and you realize that the only way to save the five people on the tracks is to throw the switch, which will turn the train onto a side track, thereby preventing it from killing the five people. However, there is a stranger standing on the side track with his back turned, and if you proceed to throw the switch, the five people will be saved, but the person on the side track will be killed.

Child

You are taking your daily walk near the train tracks and you notice that the train that is approaching is out of control. You see what has happened: the driver of the train saw five people working on the tracks and slammed on the brakes, but the brakes failed and the driver fainted. The train is now rushing toward the five people. It is moving so fast that they will not be able to get off the track in time. You happen to be standing next to a switch, and you realize that the only way to save the five people on the tracks is to throw the switch, which will turn the train onto a side track, thereby preventing it from killing the five people. However, there is a 12-year-old boy standing on the side track with his back turned, and if you proceed to throw the switch, the five people will be saved, but the boy on the side track will be killed.

We might expect men and women to have roughly the same intuitions about what the morally acceptable course of action is in these cases. As it turns out, we'd be wrong. Jennifer Zamzow and Shaun Nichols (2009) found that women are less likely than men to think that it is morally acceptable to redirect the trolley in the *Child* case, while men are less likely than women to think that it is morally acceptable to redirect the trolley in the *Stranger* case.[5] Gender diversity becomes even more pronounced when we move from ethical intuitions to epistemic intuitions and metaphysical intuitions. Wesley Buckwalter and Stephen Stich (forthcoming), for example, describe a fascinating study conducted by Christina Starmans and Ori Friedman (forthcoming). Starmans and Friedman asked people to consider the following vignette:

Watch

Peter is in his locked apartment and is reading. He decides to have a shower. He puts his book down on the coffee table. Then he takes off his watch, and also puts it on the coffee table. Then he goes into the bathroom. As Peter's shower begins, a burglar silently breaks into Peter's apartment. The burglar takes Peter's watch, puts a cheap plastic watch in its place, and then leaves. Peter has only been in the shower for two minutes, and he did not hear anything.

The results were striking: women are considerably more likely than men to say that Peter knows that there is a watch on the table.[6] Similarly striking results are found when we consider some of our metaphysical intuitions. In another study reported on by Buckwalter and Stich (forthcoming), Geoffrey Holtzman asked people to consider the following vignette:

Determined Killer
Suppose scientists figure out the exact state of the universe during the Big Bang, and figure out all the laws of physics as well. They put this information into a computer, and the computer perfectly predicts everything that has ever happened. In other words, they prove that everything that happens has to happen exactly that way because of the laws of physics and everything that's come before.

He then asked people whether it is possible for someone in this world to freely choose whether or not to murder someone else and found that women were much more likely than men to think that this was possible.[7] While future studies will be conclusive, it is beginning to seem like interpersonal intuitional diversity exists not only *between* cultures but also *within* cultures.[8]

Intuitional diversity presents a significant challenge to our intuition deploying practices. Anyone who wants to select one from among those philosophical intuitions generated in response to a specific hypothetical case will have to explain why the other intuitions should be discounted. In some cases, it won't be hard to find a plausible story to tell. As Goldman (2007) points out, there are a number of ways in which intuitions can go wrong: we might be misinformed or otherwise insufficiently informed about the case at hand; we might forget or lose track of the relevant details about the case; or our intuitive judgments about the case might be clouded by our theoretical commitments. The trouble is that, while such moves might seem plausible when we are confronted with small-scale intuitional disagreements, they seem considerably less plausible in the cases at hand, cases of large-scale systematic intuitional diversity. At the very least, it's hard to imagine how such a story would go. (In the next chapter, we will consider one rather popular story that places restrictions on whose intuitions can count as evidence.)

The alternative is to explain away our concerns about intuitional diversity. One way to do so would be to follow Goldman (2007), who argues that we should think of philosophical inquiry as aiming to help us better understand our individual or shared concepts.[9] As Goldman (2007, p. 13) writes,

> A chief attraction of [this view] is that it nicely handles challenges to the reliability of intuition arising from variability or conflicts of intuitions across persons. If the targets are construed as concepts in the personal psychological sense, then Bernard's intuition that F applies to x is evidence only for *his* personal concept of F, and Elke's intuition that F doesn't apply to x is evidence only for *her* personal concept of F. If Bernard intuits that a specified example is an instance of knowledge and Elke intuits otherwise, the conflict between intuitions can be minimized, because each bears evidentially on their own personal concepts, which may differ. This may be precisely what transpires in the cases reported by Weinberg et al.

The idea is that intuitional diversity reflects conceptual diversity, and not all kinds of conceptual diversity are necessarily problematic. But, this way of responding to intuitional diversity trades a view of philosophy as telling us something about the world for a view of philosophy as telling us something about the ways in which we think about that world and invites a shift towards certain kinds of philosophical relativism anathema to many philosophers.

3. Intuitional Sensitivity

Of course, nothing that's just been said is conclusive. In fact, we've just scratched the surface about the methodological challenges that intuitional diversity raises for our intuition deploying practices. But, that's okay because, whatever trouble intuitional diversity spells for our intuition deploying practices, diversity is not the real story here. The real story is what intuitional diversity tells us about ourselves, namely, that our philosophical intuitions might be sensitive to things we hadn't anticipated (and in ways that our philosophical theories haven't accounted for). This comes across most clearly when we turn our attention from *interpersonal* intuitional diversity to *intrapersonal* intuitional diversity – that is, from intuitional differences between people to intuitional differences within people.

One particularly interesting kind of *intrapersonal* intuitional diversity results from an apparent intuitional sensitivity to the presence or absence of *affective content* in the description of certain hypothetical cases. We saw an example of this in Chapter 2; recall that Shaun Nichols and Joshua Knobe (2007) found that people have different intuitions about the relationship between causal determinism and moral responsibility depending on whether or not the hypothetical case they are evaluating has affective content. Of course, this kind of intuitional sensitivity is not limited to metaphysical intuitions. Eric Uhlmann, David Pizarro, David Tannenbaum, and Peter Ditto (2009) recently found that some *moral* intuitions also show sensitivity to affectively charged content.[10] In one study, Uhlmann and his colleagues asked people to consider two versions of Judith Jarvis Thomson's (1985) *Fat Man* case:

> *Fat Man*
> Consider a case – which I shall call *Fat Man* – in which you are standing on a footbridge over the trolley track. You can see a trolley hurtling down the track, out of control. You turn around to see where the trolley is headed, and there are five workmen on the track where it exits from under the footbridge. What to do? Being an expert on trolleys, you know of one certain way to stop an out-of-control trolley: Drop a really heavy weight in its path. But where to find one? It just so happens that standing next to you on the footbridge is a fat man, a really fat man. He is leaning over the railing, watching the trolley; all you have to do is give him a little shove, and over the railing he will go, onto the track in the path of the trolley. Would it be permissible for you to do this?

Some people were asked to consider a version of this case in which an agent could choose to sacrifice an individual named "Chip Ellsworth III" to save 100 members of the Harlem Jazz Orchestra, while other people were asked to consider a version of the case in which the agent could choose to sacrifice an individual named "Tyrone Payton" to save 100 members of the New York

Philharmonic. Remarkably, people (especially people who identified themselves as politically liberal) were more likely to think that it is morally permissible to sacrifice Chip Ellsworth III than they were to think that it is morally permissible to sacrifice Tyrone Payton.[11] One explanation for this asymmetrical result is that people who identify themselves as politically liberal tend to demonstrate a significant aversion to adopting attitudes that might be considered prejudiced (Plant & Devine 1998, Monin & Miller 2001, Norton et al. 2004). This aversion to even the appearance of prejudice, when combined with the different racial undertones of the two cases, causes people (especially people who identify themselves as politically liberal) to have different emotional responses to the two cases – emotional responses that, in turn, trigger different moral intuitions.[12]

We have seen that philosophical intuitions are sensitive to cultural background, gender, and the presence or absence of affective content in the description of the hypothetical case. Recently, Stacey Swain, Joshua Alexander, and Jonathan Weinberg (2008) found yet another form of intuitional sensitivity: sensitivity to the context in which the hypothetical case is being considered. In particular, they found that subjects have different epistemic intuitions depending on whether, and which, other hypothetical cases are considered first. Consider, for example, the following version of Keith Lehrer's *Truetemp* case:

Truetemp
One day Charles was knocked out by a falling rock; as a result his brain was "rewired" so that he is always right whenever he estimates the temperature where he is. Charles is unaware that his brain has been altered in this way. A few weeks later, this brain rewiring leads him to believe that it is 71 degrees in his room. Apart from his estimation, he has no other reasons to think that it is 71 degrees. In fact, it is 71 degrees.

Some people were asked to consider the *Truetemp* case before evaluating any other hypothetical case. Others were asked to evaluate the *Truetemp* case after considering a clear case of knowledge:

Karen is a distinguished professor of chemistry. This morning, she read in an article in a leading scientific journal that mixing two common floor disinfectants, Cleano Plus and Washaway, will create a poisonous gas that is deadly to humans. In fact, the article is correct: mixing the two products does create a poisonous gas. At noon, Karen sees a janitor mixing Cleano Plus and Washaway and yells to him, "Get away! Mixing those two products creates a poisonous gas!"

And, still others were asked to evaluate the *Truetemp* case after being asked to evaluate a clear case of non-knowledge:

Dave likes to play a game with flipping a coin. He sometimes gets a "special feeling" that the next flip will come out heads. When he gets this "special feeling", he is right about half the time, and wrong about half the time. Just before the next flip, Dave gets that "special feeling", and the feeling leads him to believe that the coin will land heads. He flips the coin, and it does land heads.

We found that, when compared with people who were asked to evaluate the *Truetemp* case before evaluating any other cases, people who were asked to evaluate the *Truetemp* case after first being asked to evaluate a clear case of knowledge were less willing to attribute knowledge in the *Truetemp* case, and people who were asked to evaluate the *Truetemp* case after first being asked to evaluate a clear case of non-knowledge were more willing to attribute knowledge in the *Truetemp* case.[13] This suggests that *Truetemp* intuitions are being influenced by the context in which the hypothetical case is being considered.

Psychologists have been aware of this kind of intuitional sensitivity for some time. In an earlier study, Lewis Petrinovich and Patricia O'Neill (1996) found that some of our moral intuitions also show sensitivity to order and context. They had people consider three versions of the *Trolley* case.[14] The first version was as follows:

Switch
A trolley is hurtling down the tracks. There are five innocent people on the track ahead of the trolley, and they will be killed if the trolley continues going straight ahead. There is a spur of track leading off to the side. There is one innocent person on that spur of track. The brakes of the trolley have failed and there is a switch that can be activated to cause the trolley to go to the side track.

You are an innocent bystander (that is, not an employee of the railroad, etc.). You can throw the switch, saving five innocent people, which will result in the death of the one innocent person on the side track. What would you do?

The second and third versions differed only in the placement of the innocent person and the action that would be required to save the five track workers. In the second version – let's call this the *Button* case – the innocent person is on a bridge above the tracks and the action required in order to save the track workers involves pushing a button that would cause a ramp to go underneath the trolley causing, in turn, the trolley to jump the tracks onto the bridge, killing the innocent person but saving the five track workers. In the third version – let's call this the *Push* case – the innocent person is on a bridge with you and the action required in order to save the track workers involves pushing the innocent person onto the tracks into the path of the trolley. Petrinovich and O'Neill asked some people to consider these cases in the order just presented (*Switch – Button – Push*) and others to consider these cases in the reverse order (*Push – Button – Switch*). They found that people were more willing to act to save the five track workers in both the *Switch* case and the *Push* case when those cases appeared first in the sequence than when they appeared last in the sequence,[15] and that people were more willing to act to save the five track workers in the *Button* case when that case followed the *Switch* case than when it followed the *Push* case.[16] This suggests that our intuitions about these cases, like our intuitions about the *Truetemp* case, are sensitive to the context in which those cases are being considered.[17]

Philosophical intuitions, it turns out, are sensitive to a host of things we hadn't expected them to be sensitive to (to facts about who is considering the relevant hypothetical case, the presence or absence of certain kinds of content, and the context in which the hypothetical case is being considered) and this sensitivity produces both *inter*personal and *intra*personal intuitional diversity. As we will see, intuitional sensitivity – particularly, unanticipated and unwelcome intuitional sensitivity – presents a different kind of challenge to our intuition deploying practices and the future success of those practices will depend on our ability to come to better understand and accommodate these forms of intuitional sensitivity.

4. Restrictionism Explained

These studies don't provide the last word, but they do strongly suggest that some philosophical intuitions are sensitive to cultural background, gender, affectivity, and context. Sensitivity alone is not problematic. We want our evidence to be sensitive, but we want it to be sensitive to the right kinds of things. In particular, we want our evidence to be sensitive only to those things that we think are relevant to the truth or falsity of the set of claims for which the evidence is supposed to provide evidence. What makes this kind of intuitional sensitivity *problematic*, then, is that it is *unwelcome*: some philosophical intuitions, it seems, are sensitive to things that most philosophers don't want them to be – or at least, haven't wanted them to be. Most philosophers don't think that the truth or falsity of claims about knowledge or meaning depends on facts about who is evaluating the relevant hypothetical cases. Most philosophers don't think that the truth or falsity of claims about moral responsibility or morally right action depends on whether or not our affective states have been engaged. And most philosophers don't think that the truth or falsity of claims about knowledge or moral responsibility depends on the context in which those claims are evaluated. Of course, the fact that these things haven't traditionally been taken to be relevant to the truth or falsity of philosophical claims doesn't mean that they are, in fact, irrelevant.[18] Philosophers might just be wrong about what is relevant to the truth or falsity of philosophical claims. But, it does put pressure on our intuition deploying practices. At the very least, philosophers face a dilemma: either we must explain why these kinds of intuitional sensitivity are welcome or we must stop appealing to these philosophical intuitions as evidence and place *local restrictions* on our intuition deploying practices. (The name "restrictionism" derives from the second horn of this dilemma.)

Whatever option we choose, the challenge to our intuition deploying practices doesn't end there. Not only is this kind of intuitional sensitivity unwelcome, it was *unexpected*. Even now, we lack the means to predict when or where else this kind of intuitional sensitivity will appear, and find ourselves in the untenable epistemic position of suspecting that *some* intuitional evidence is problematically sensitive without being able to reliably predict *what* intuitional evidence is problematically sensitive.

Jonathan Weinberg (2007) calls this kind of epistemic position "hopeless", but not *hopelessly* so. We lack the ability to detect and correct problematic intuitional sensitivity, but this condition need not be permanent. According to Weinberg, four things contribute to hope: external corroboration (agreement *between* sources of evidence); internal coherence (agreement *within* sources of evidence); detectability of margins (awareness of a source's limits); and theoretical illumination (awareness of how sources work when they do and why they don't when they don't). If intuitions aren't hopelessly hopeless, the question becomes what we can do to restore hope.

Ernest Sosa (2007a) has suggested that maybe we just need to be more careful. Drawing on the comparison between intuitional evidence and perceptual evidence, Sosa writes,

> [S]urely the effects of priming, framing, and other such contextual factors will affect the epistemic status of intuition in general, only in the sort of way that they affect the epistemic status of perceptual observation in general. One would think that the ways of preserving the epistemic importance of perception in the face of such effects on perceptual judgments would be analogously available for the preservation of the epistemic importance of intuition in the face of such effects on intuitive judgments. The upshot is that we have to be *careful* in how we use intuitions, not that intuition is useless. (p. 105)

The idea is that we should treat worries about the epistemic standing of philosophical intuitions in the same way that we treat worries about the epistemic standing of perceptions. We know that perceptions are problematically sensitive too (think, for example, of perceptual illusion or hallucination) and yet we don't think that our perception deploying practices are significantly challenged by this fact. Instead, we are careful about what perceptual evidence we use and when we use it.

It pays to be careful, but only when we know what it means to be careful, and here is where the analogy between intuitional evidence and perceptual evidence breaks down. We have a pretty good understanding of when sense perception goes wrong, something that is reflected in our perceptual practices and reinforced by a communal scientific understanding of the mechanisms responsible for our perceptual judgments. This prevents worries about problematic perceptual sensitivity from giving rise to global concerns about the epistemic standing of perceptual evidence. The problem is that we aren't in the same position with respect to intuitional evidence. Our inability to predict or explain problematic intuitional sensitivity puts us in a different epistemic position with respect to intuitions than we are in with respect to perception. In a sense, we haven't learned yet what it would mean to be careful. Learning how to be careful means developing a better understanding of how intuitions work. If we are going to learn *what* intuitional evidence can be used and *when* intuitional evidence can be used, our intuition deploying practices must be informed by an understanding of the relevant psychology, cognitive science, and an empirically informed philosophy of mind. We need to know more about where philosophical intuitions come from, what mechanisms are responsible for producing them, and what factors influence them. Only then will it be possible to exercise greater care in our intuition deploying practices.

5. Restrictionism Defended: Lessons from the Past

This is not the first time our intuition deploying practices have been challenged, and it is worth asking what lessons the restrictionist challenge has learned from those that came before it. One thing that we've learned from previous challenges to our intuition deploying practices is that a successful challenge shouldn't rest on too narrow a conception of philosophy. Hilary Kornblith (1998, 2002, 2007) has famously argued that philosophical intuitions simply aren't particularly important to our philosophical practices, or at least aren't as important as many philosophers suggest. The idea is that, since our philosophical intuitions only provide evidence about our individual or shared concepts, and since philosophers shouldn't be particularly interested in such things (or at least their interest shouldn't be limited to such things), philosophical intuitions don't have a significant role to play in philosophical practice. This isn't to say that they have *no* role in philosophical practice. Kornblith allows that they can serve as starting-points that inform the direction of our early philosophical investigations; but these starting-points should "give way to more straightforwardly empirical investigations of external phenomena" (Kornblith 1998, p. 135). The problem with this way of challenging philosophy's intuition deploying practices is that it rests on too narrow a conception of philosophy. Of course, some philosophers aren't interested in our concepts of things but in the things themselves, and Kornblith might be right that philosophical intuitions don't have a significant role (or at least as significant a role) to play in philosophical discussions of the non-psychological world. But, other philosophers are interested in our concepts of things, and rightly so. This interest might be coupled with an interest in things themselves together with the view that only by first understanding our concepts of things can we begin to understand things themselves. This interest might also be entirely divorced from an interest in the non-psychological world, focusing instead on the meaning of our philosophical concepts or on the psychological mechanisms that are responsible for our conceptual judgments. In either case, even if it turned out that our philosophical intuitions were not particularly important for philosophical projects unconcerned with our concepts of things, more would be needed to demonstrate that they are philosophically insignificant full stop.

Another thing that we've learned from earlier challenges to our intuition deploying practices is that a successful challenge shouldn't be so strong that it threatens to undermine *all* of our evidential practices. Let's look at two examples. The first example concerns the fallibility of philosophical intuitions, and can be treated rather quickly. Michael Devitt (1994) and Catherine Elgin (1996) both argue that philosophical intuitions cannot be treated as evidence because they are fallible. The problem with this move should be clear: all putative sources of evidence are fallible, so this move would lead to *global* skepticism. Since most of us think that global skepticism should be avoided, we can't rule out intuitional evidence, or any other kind of evidence, just because it's fallible. The second example concerns the reliability of philosophical intuitions, or more precisely how we come to *believe* that they are reliable. Robert Cummins (1998) argues that philosophical intuitions cannot be treated as evidence because we have no independent justification for thinking that they are reliable guides to the truth. We cannot establish that philosophical intuitions are reliable without relying on philosophical intuitions. Setting aside any concerns that we might have with epistemic internalism, the problem with this move is that it also leads to global skepticism (Pust 2000, Goldman 2007). To see why, let's start with perception. The most natural way to establish the reliability of perception is by offering some sort of inductive argument over past accurate perceptions, but this kind of inductive argument relies on measuring perceptions against one another. We are, in effect, using perception to establish its own reliability. The same is true for introspection, and arguably for any of our basic sources of evidence. We cannot establish the reliability of any of our basic sources of evidence without relying on other basic sources of evidence, so if some kind of epistemic bootstrapping isn't permitted, then it seems like more than just our intuition deploying practices are put in jeopardy.

There is another lesson to be learned from worries about epistemic bootstrapping, namely, that a successful challenge to our intuition deploying practices shouldn't demand the epistemically impossible. Consider, again, the idea that philosophical intuitions cannot be treated as evidence unless we have independent justification for thinking that they are reliable guides to the truth. As already observed, the most natural way to establish the reliability of a putative source of evidence is by offering some sort of inductive argument over past accurate reports made by that source of evidence. Unless we allow some kind of epistemic bootstrapping, this requires that we check the reports of that putative source of evidence against the reports of another putative source of evidence. So, if we are trying to establish the reliability of philosophical intuitions in a way that avoids epistemic bootstrapping, we must appeal to some putative source of evidence other than philosophical intuition − call this putative source of evidence E_1. Of course, the constraint that we cannot treat something as evidence until we have established its reliability applies no less to E_1 than to intuition. As such, if we are to appeal to E_1 in order to establish the reliability of philosophical intuition, we must first establish the reliability of E_1 and do so on the basis of some other putative source of evidence − call this putative source of evidence E_2. It should be easy to see the problem that emerges. We are charged with a task that we cannot complete. We can't treat philosophical intuitions as evidence until we've established their reliability; but, in order to establish the reliability of *any* given putative source of evidence, we have to have already established the reliability of *some* (other) putative source of evidence. This cannot be done.

We have a sense for some of the problems faced by earlier attempts to challenge our intuition deploying practices. These provide some guidelines for what a successful challenge must look like: it shouldn't rest on too narrow a conception of philosophy; it shouldn't be so strong that it threatens global skepticism; and it should demand the epistemically impossible. How well, then, has experimental restrictionism learned these lessons? Pretty well, it seems. While experimental restrictionism might seem to *motivate* a move towards one particular conception of philosophy, namely, one that treats our philosophical intuitions as telling us only about our individual or shared concepts, it is not *motivated* by any particular conception of philosophy. What's more, experimental restrictionism seems neither to invite global skepticism by threatening the status of our other evidential practices nor to demand the epistemically impossible. Most of our evidential practices are hopeful, and so don't face the same methodological challenges that our intuition deploying practices currently face. With most of our evidential practices, we have a fairly good sense of what evidence to use and when to use it, and so the methodological challenges faced by our intuition deploying practices are fairly localized to those practices. And, far from being impossible, the methodological prescriptions endorsed by restrictionists aren't even epistemically unreasonable: we are simply called to reconcile our views about philosophy, philosophical evidence, and our intuition deploying practices with the existence of certain kinds of intuitional sensitivity; and asked to spend more time and energy thinking carefully about the nature of intuitional evidence, where it comes from, what mechanisms are responsible for producing it, and what factors influence it.

6. Conclusion

We have a sense of the problem, and of the challenge it presents for our intuition deploying practices. Some of our intuitional evidence is sensitive to things we neither expected nor perhaps wanted it to be; in response, we must either explain away the problem by welcoming this kind of intuitional sensitivity or enact local restrictions on what kinds of intuitional evidence to use and when to use it. Either option, it seems, requires that we spend more time thinking hard about not only philosophical practice but also about the nature of ourselves and our philosophical intuitions. And, this means that either option is going to require more experimental philosophy.

5

In Defense of Experimental Philosophy

1. Introduction

Calls for change are often met with resistance, especially by those heavily invested in the orthodox. It is perhaps unsurprising, then, that experimental philosophy has not been universally well received. Philosophers invested in more traditional ways of thinking about philosophy and philosophical methodology have not gone quietly into that good night, but instead have attempted to mount a number of defenses of the tradition. In this chapter, we will focus on three of the more common strategies employed by philosophers in defense of the tradition. (There are other ways of defending the tradition, including challenging experimental philosophy on methodological grounds. We will examine methodological challenges in the epilogue.) These strategies take aim at the work done by experimental philosophers, and involve arguing that this work is *irrelevant* either because it focuses on the wrong kinds of philosophical intuitions or because it focuses too much on philosophical intuitions.

2. Whose Intuitions Matter?

Maybe not all philosophical intuitions are created equal. This rather straightforward idea has become increasingly attractive, in part because it seems to offer an equally straightforward response to experimental philosophy. The response goes something like this. Whatever it is that experimental philosophers have been studying, they haven't been studying the kind of intuitional evidence relevant to philosophy's intuition deploying practices, and so the results of such studies have little to say about or to contribute to those practices.

One particularly popular version of this response has become known as the *expertise defense*.[1] According to the expertise defense, our interest in philosophical intuitions should be understood to be an interest in *philosophers'* intuitions. Kirk Ludwig (2007) provides a wonderfully straightforward articulation of the expertise defense in his discussion of the role played by philosophical intuitions in the philosophy of language:

> We should not expect antecedently that untrained subjects should be in an especially good position to give judgments in response to scenarios involving difficult questions about the semantics of proper names, for this is a domain of considerable complexity where our ordinary vocabulary is not especially precise. We should instead expect that the relevant experts in the field of philosophical semantics will be better placed to give answers which focus on the right features of the cases and what they are supposed to be responding to . . . What is called for is the development of a discipline in which general expertise in the conduct of thought experiments is inculcated and in which expertise in different fields of conceptual inquiry is developed and refined. There is such a discipline. It is called philosophy. Philosophers are best suited by training and expertise to conduct thought experiments in their areas of expertise and to sort out the methodological and conceptual issues that arise in trying to get clear about the complex structure of concepts with which we confront the world. (pp. 150–1)

Education and experience are also emphasized by Steven Hales (2006), who writes:

Intuitions are and should be sensitive to education and training in the relevant domain. For example, the physical intuitions
of professional scientists are much more trustworthy than those
of undergraduates or random persons in a bus station. Scientists
have and rely on physical intuitions, intuitions that are trained,
educated, and informed and yet are good indicators of truth for
those very reasons. In the same way, the modal intuitions of professional philosophers are much more reliable than either those of
inexperienced students or the "folk". (p. 171)

The common thought seems to be this. We should be interested in
expert philosophical intuitions rather than folk philosophical intuitions. After all, philosophers have better concepts and theories, or
at least a better understanding of the relevant concepts and theories,
have thought long and hard about these concepts and theories, and
have been trained in how best to read and think about philosophical thought experiments that call upon us to apply these concepts
and theories. Surely, this makes expert philosophical intuitions more
theoretically valuable than folk philosophical intuitions.

While this is an attractive idea, it turns out to be quite difficult
to determine who has expertise about what and when. It seems that
only certain kinds of training help improve task performance and,
even then, only for certain kinds of tasks, and there is reason to worry
that philosophical training doesn't seem to be the right kind of training nor does philosophical thought-experimenting seem to be the
right kind of task (see, e.g., Shanteau 1992, Ericsson et al. 2006, and,
for discussion, Weinberg et al. 2010). So, we can't simply assume
that expert philosophical intuitions are more theoretically valuable
than folk philosophical intuitions. Instead, we must carefully examine
what reasons we might have for thinking that they should be.

One reason that we might have for thinking that expert philosophical intuitions are more theoretically valuable than folk philosophical
intuitions is that philosophers have better concepts and theories, or
at least a better understanding of the relevant concepts and theories.
Peter Singer (1972) advances this view in his discussion of moral
expertise, writing:

[I]t would seem that the moral philosopher does have some
important advantages over the ordinary man ... his specific

experience in moral philosophy gives him an understanding of moral concepts and of the logic of moral argument. The possibility of serious confusion arising if one engages in moral argument without a clear understanding of the concepts employed has been sufficiently emphasized in recent moral philosophy and does not need to be demonstrated here. Clarity is not an end in itself, but it is an aid to sound argument, and the need for clarity is something which moral philosophers have recognised. (p. 117)

Hilary Kornblith (2007) also emphasizes the benefit of having appropriate theoretical understanding, writing:

Theory-informed judgments in science may be more telling than the judgments of the uninformed because accurate background theory leads to more accurate theory-informed judgment. The uninformed observer and the sophisticated scientist are each trying to capture an independently existing phenomenon, and accurate background theory aids in that task. Experts are better observers than the uninitiated. If the situation of philosophical theory construction is analogous, as I believe it is, then we should see philosophers as attempting to characterize, not their concepts, let alone the concepts of the folk, but certain extra-mental phenomena, such as knowledge, justification, the good, the right, and so on. The intuitions of professional philosophers are better in getting at these phenomena than the intuitions of the folk because philosophers have thought long and hard about the phenomena, and their concepts, if all is working as it should, come closer to accurately characterizing the phenomena under study than those of the naïve. (p. 35)

Let's begin with the idea that philosophical expertise consists in having better concepts or at least better conceptual understanding. There are several ways of cashing this idea out. One way is to suggest that philosophical discussions typically involve *technical* concepts, and that philosophers have privileged access to these concepts by virtue of their philosophical education. The problem with this suggestion is that it simply doesn't seem to be true to say that most philosophical discussions involve technical concepts.[2] There are certainly some philosophical discussions that do; philosophical discussions about the nature of *validity* or *warranted assertability* come to mind. But many philosophical discussions involve rather ordinary concepts, and for good reason. Concerns about these ordinary concepts are precisely what gave rise to these philosophical discussions in the first place. If these discussions were then couched in purely technical terms, they would lose traction with the ordinary concerns that gave rise to them. It's hard to see, for example, how a philosophical discussion about some purely technical concept of knowledge could ever hope to tell us much about the kinds of epistemic worries involving our ordinary concept that motivate much of contemporary epistemology.

If philosophical expertise doesn't consist in having better concepts, maybe it consists in having a better understanding of ordinary concepts.[3] Maybe philosophers are able to make more precise conceptual distinctions, for example. While this might make expert philosophical intuitions more theoretically valuable than folk philosophical intuitions, it is important to note that questions about comparative conceptual competence are precisely the kinds of questions that experimental philosophy might seem well suited to help us investigate. As Joshua Knobe and Shaun Nichols (2008) write:

> This version of the expertise objection argument brings up a number of fascinating issues, but we don't see how it even begins to serve as an objection to the practice of experimental philosophy. On the contrary, we would love to know more about the ways in which philosophers differ from ordinary folks, and it seems to us that the best way to find out would be to run some experiments . . . Furthermore, even if we discover important differences between the philosophers and the folk, it would hardly follow that data from the folk are irrelevant. Rather, the whole pattern of data might tell us something important about the ultimate source of the philosophical problems. (p. 9)

In short, the suggestion that philosophers have a better understanding of ordinary concepts invites *more* experimental work on our philosophical intuitions, not less.

It also invites a question. Evidence that philosophers have a different understanding of ordinary concepts isn't evidence that they have a better understanding of those concepts, so why might we think that they do? The answer typically has something to do with philosophical education – philosophical education somehow improves our conceptual understanding. But, it is not clear exactly how this is supposed to happen. Jonathan Weinberg, Chad Gonnerman, Cameron Buckner, and Joshua Alexander (2010) suggest that most philosophers think it happens via some process of trial and error, where philosophy students train their conceptual competencies by checking their conceptual judgments against some received standard. One hypothesis is that philosophy students train their conceptual judgments against previously certified philosophical intuitions, but this only invites explanatory regress. How were *those* philosophical intuitions certified? Another hypothesis is that philosophy students train their conceptual judgments against established philosophical theory, but again this invites explanatory regress. If philosophy students are supposed to train their philosophical intuitions against established philosophical theories, and expert philosophical intuitions play a substantial role in establishing those theories, we are still left wondering how expert philosophical intuitions are certified. The worry, of course, is that our philosophical intuitions don't receive anything like the kind of objective feedback that would seem necessary in order to actually help us *improve* our conceptual understanding. In fact, matters get even worse. As Weinberg et al. (2010) explain,

> [V]arious of the psychological mechanisms that can plague human cognition in general – overgeneralization, overconfidence, cognitive dissonance, attribution error, belief bias, belief perseverance, and so on – might very well lead philosophers to believe that we have attuned intuitions, even if in reality in many places we have simply been systematically reaffirming early impressions and incorrectly attributing our professional successes (e.g., in debate and publication) to their validity. (p. 341)

Not only do we have reason to worry that philosophical education isn't particularly helpful, we have reason to worry that we aren't particularly well adapted to realize this.

Perhaps philosophical expertise consists in having mastered some set of philosophical theories and principles. Hilary Kornblith (2007) has something like this in mind when he writes,

Intuitions uninformed by any theory – or only minimally informed by theories common to the folk – would be no more useful [in philosophy] than observations performed by investigators wholly ignorant of relevant background theory in science. We do not go out of our way, in the sciences, to have observations made by individuals so ignorant of relevant theory that their corpus of beliefs contain no theories at all which might threaten to affect those observations . . . The suggestion that we should attempt to capture pre-theoretical intuition . . . seems to privilege the intuitions of the ignorant and the naïve over those of responsible and well-informed investigators. I cannot see why this would be a better idea in philosophy than it is in science. (p. 34)

The idea seems to be that philosophical theories can help shape our intuitions, perhaps by helping to make certain features of a given hypothetical case salient or by guiding our interpretation of those features.[4] While this is an appealing suggestion, it faces several difficulties. First, judgments filtered through philosophical theory might not even count as philosophical *intuitions*; at the very least, the filtering process would have to be unconscious or otherwise introspectively opaque in order for the subsequent judgments to count as genuine philosophical intuitions on some accounts (e.g., Lynch 2006). Second, theoretical commitments are just as likely to contaminate as they are to clarify. The fact that expert philosophical intuitions are theoretically informed doesn't ensure that they are *more* theoretically valuable than folk philosophical intuitions; in fact, they might be *less* theoretically valuable for that very reason. Kornblith recognizes this possibility, but argues that this simply means that we need to do whatever we can to make sure that the theories that influence our philosophical intuitions are accurate. It is not clear, though, what this would mean for philosophy's intuition deploying practices. If our theoretical commitments shape our philosophical intuitions, it is hard to see how our philosophical intuitions can help us *independently* assess the accuracy of those theories. This isn't a problem for someone like Kornblith, who thinks that our intuition deploying practices have quite limited philosophical value. But, it does present a significant challenge to anyone who thinks that we advance philosophical theories on the basis of their ability to explain our philosophical intuitions, defend their truth on the basis of their overall agreement with our philosophical intuitions, and justify our philosophical beliefs on the basis of their accordance with our philosophical intuitions.

Let's switch gears a bit. Maybe philosophical expertise simply consists in the fact that philosophers spend more time thinking carefully about philosophical issues. Antti Kauppinen (2007) adopts something like this position when he argues that *robust* philosophical intuitions are more theoretically valuable than *surface* philosophical intuitions. One mark of robust philosophical intuitions is that they are formed in *sufficiently ideal conditions*, conditions in which we have the time to carefully examine and evaluate not only our judgments about hypothetical cases, but also the cases themselves and what influence our philosophical commitments might have on what details we find relevant in those cases.[5] The underlying thought is that *reflective* judgments have a better chance of being right (see, e.g., Sosa 1991) and so, if philosophers spend more time engaged in this kind of reflective practice, then it might seem natural to think that their philosophical intuitions are more theoretically valuable than folk philosophical intuitions.

As Hilary Kornblith (2002, 2010) and Jonathan Weinberg and Joshua Alexander (forthcoming) point out, however, the relationship between reflection and reliability is not this straightforward. True, there are times when reflection helps improve our judgments. Reflection can sometimes help us to realize that we had been misinformed or uninformed about some relevant detail of the particular case, that we had lost track of some of the relevant details, or that our initial judgments about what details are relevant were contaminated by our theoretical commitments. But, reflection can just as easily serve as an echo chamber, simply ratifying whatever initial judgments we might have made. It can help increase our confidence in those judgments without increasing their reliability. One problem is that the cognitive processes involved in the formation of our conceptual judgments aren't introspectively accessible (Nisbett & Wilson 1977, Wilson 2002).[6] Another is that we tend to be overconfident in our own reliability; we overestimate the degree to which our beliefs are based on the relevant details and underestimate the degree to which our decisions about what details are relevant are contaminated by our theoretical commitments. Perhaps the biggest problem, however, is that when we actually attempt to engage in the kind of reflection that Kauppinen has in mind, a host of cognitive biases are likely to get in the way (see, e.g., Wason 1960, Nickerson 1998, and Baron 2000). In fact, even being aware of this won't help, since we tend to do a particularly bad job of compensating for even known cognitive biases (Pronin et al. 2002). In short, it is far from obvious that reflection helps enough to support the claim that expert philosophical intuitions are more theoretically valuable than folk philosophical intuitions.[7]

There is another possibility; maybe philosophical expertise consists in some kind of *procedural* knowledge – some special "know-how" developed over the course of our philosophical education. If philosophers are better trained in how best to read and think about philosophical thought experiments, this might naturally make their philosophical intuitions seem more theoretically valuable than folk philosophical intuitions. So, what might this procedural expertise look like? Here are two possibilities. Ernest Sosa (2009) has recently observed that the vignettes typically used in philosophical thought experiments require the reader to import a certain amount of information not explicitly contained in the passage itself. In this way, reading philosophical thought experiments is similar to reading fiction:[8]

> When we read fiction we import a great deal that is not explicit in the text. We import a lot that is normally presupposed about the physical and social structure construction as we follow the author's lead in our own imaginative construction. (p. 107)

If this is right, then we might construe philosophical procedural expertise in terms of our ability to properly get at the relevant details of a particular vignette, our ability to appropriately fill in details not explicitly contained in the vignette, and our ability to entertain these details in our imaginations. Timothy Williamson (2007, 2011) suggests a different kind of procedural expertise. On Williamson's account, thought experiments involve deductively valid arguments with counterfactual premises, and we are supposed to evaluate them using a mixture of imaginative simulation, background information, and logic. Williamson (2011) attempts to decompose the task of thought experimenting into discernible sub-tasks: we must read and digest the description of the scenario, judge what would be the case in the scenario described, judge whether the scenario is possible, and determine whether the premises entail the conclusion. If this reconstruction of the process of thinking about thought experiments is right, then we might construe philosophical procedural expertise in terms of our ability to pick out the relevant details of a particular vignette, engage in counterfactual reasoning, and make certain logical inferences. Both of these seem like fairly interesting pictures of what philosophical expertise might look like, but it is important to see that questions about comparative procedural expertise, like questions of comparative conceptual competence, are precisely the kinds of questions that experimental philosophy should be well suited to help us investigate. So, it is hard to transform the possibility that philosophers have greater procedural know-how into a reason to diminish the philosophical significance of experimental philosophy.

We have examined a number of reasons why we might think that expert philosophical intuitions are more theoretically valuable than folk philosophical intuitions: philosophers have better concepts and theories, or at least a better understanding of the relevant concepts and theories, have thought long and hard about these concepts and theories, and have been trained in how best to read and think about philosophical thought experiments that call upon us to apply these concepts and theories. None are particularly persuasive, at least at this point. At the very least, more work needs to be done to explain why we should think that expert philosophical intuitions are more theoretically valuable than folk philosophical intuitions. Much of this work is likely going to have to be empirical, and is going to involve carefully studying folk philosophical intuitions, expert philosophical intuitions, and the cognitive processes involved in thinking about philosophical thought experiments and generating philosophical intuitions.[9]

3. What Intuitions Matter?

Of course, there are other ways of trying to reduce the significance of experimental philosophy. One increasingly popular way has been to shift our attention from *whose* intuitions are relevant to *what* intuitions are relevant. Jonathan Weinberg and Joshua Alexander (forthcoming) call this the *thickness defense* because it typically involves adopting one or another of the thick conceptions of philosophical intuition outlined in Chapter 1. The basic strategy of the thickness defense is to argue that, whatever it is that philosophical intuitions are, they are not the kind of thing that can be studied using the kinds of experimental studies that have been stock-in-trade for experimental philosophers. Kirk Ludwig (2007) provides a particularly clear example of the thickness defense:[10]

> The first point to make is that . . . responses to surveys about scenarios used in thought experiments are not *ipso facto* intuitions, that is, they are not *ipso facto* judgments which express solely the subject's competence in the deployment of the concepts involved in them in response to the scenario . . . The task when presented with responses which we know are not (at least all) intuitions is to try to factor out the contribution of competencies from the other factors. This requires an understanding of what the various factors are that may influence responses and enough information about each subject to be able to say with some confidence what factors are at work. It is clear that in the circumstances in which these surveys are conducted we do not have this kind of information. (pp. 144–5)

The basic idea is that, because not all survey responses reveal our philosophical intuitions, experimental philosophers inherit the burden of distinguishing philosophical intuitions from other kinds of mental states that might be revealed by those responses, a burden that their methods currently prevent them from being able to discharge.

This is an attractive strategy, especially when faced with the kind of methodological challenge rehearsed in the previous chapter. If experimental philosophers haven't been studying the right kind of thing, then whatever methodological worries they've raised aren't worries about the *actual* methods used in philosophical practice. As Weinberg and Alexander (forthcoming) point out, however, this strategy only works if certain conditions have been met, conditions having to do with the propensity of philosophical intuitions to track the truth and with our ability to successfully identify in practice which of our mental states count as genuine philosophical intuitions.[11] If it turned out that philosophical intuitions were no more likely to track philosophical truth than the kinds of mental states studied by experimental philosophers, then there would be little comfort in finding out that experimental philosophers haven't been studying philosophical intuitions all along. Likewise, there would be little comfort in knowing that experimental philosophers haven't been studying the right kind of mental states unless we have the resources needed to pick those mental states out in actual philosophical practice. And the problem is that no version of the thickness defense *clearly* meets both conditions. The problem with some versions is that they simply don't provide the goods, treating philosophical intuitions in such a way that we either have good reason to worry that they won't track philosophical truth or else lack the means to distinguish them from other kinds of mental states. But, the more common problem is that most versions of the thickness defense simply leave it open whether or not the conditions have been met. And this means that more experimental work will be needed, not less, even if that experimental work needs to take greater care to determine that the right kinds of mental states are being studied.

4. Do Intuitions Matter?

Maybe the issue isn't *whose* intuitions matter, or even *what* intuitions matter, but *whether* intuitions matter at all. Experimental philosophers adopt the view that philosophical intuitions play a significant role in contemporary philosophy, providing data to be explained by our philosophical theories, evidence that those theories are true, and reasons for believing them to be true. This is true even for those experimental philosophers who think that learning more about how our minds work and how we think about philosophical issues raises concerns about the role that intuitions play in philosophical practice. In short, experimental philosophers take philosophical intuitions seriously, and this means that the philosophical significance of experimental philosophy depends, at least in part, on the significance of our philosophical intuitions. If it turned out that our intuitions weren't philosophically significant, then experimental philosophy would be left to occupy the unhappy position of taking seriously a way of thinking about philosophy not worthy of serious consideration in the first place – it would be philosophically insignificant.

Along these lines, it has become increasingly popular to argue that philosophical intuitions don't play a significant role in contemporary philosophy. Max Deutsch (2010) advances this view, arguing that, while *counterexamples* play a significant role in contemporary philosophy, our intuitions about these counterexamples do not. According to Deutsch, whether someone has the intuition that a given counterexample is true is purely a psychological matter, and forgetting this fact is precisely what allows experimental philosophers to gain purchase in discussions of philosophical methodology. Jonathan Ichikawa (forthcoming) also resists the view that contemporary philosophy relies on our philosophical intuitions, arguing that, while philosophers rely on *intuitive propositions*, it is a mistake to think that this means that they are relying on intuitions as evidence or even that they are relying on intuitive propositions because they are intuitive. According to Ichikawa, when philosophers appeal to the intuitive nature of certain propositions, they are attempting to make a dialectical move, not an evidential one.

Whether philosophical intuitions *do* play a significant role in contemporary philosophy is a sociological matter, and a great deal depends both on how we interpret appeals to *what we would say* or *how things seem to us to be*, and on what sort of move we think is being made when philosophers appeal to such things. We will discuss the second issue in a little while, but before we do it is worth spending a moment talking about the way that philosophers talk about intuitions. Deutsch (2010), for example, argues that philosophical intuitions don't play a significant role in philosophy because most philosophical discussions simply don't include explicit appeal to our philosophical intuitions, even those discussions that are often treated as paradigmatic examples of the central role that philosophical intuitions are supposed to play in philosophical practice.[12] This move seems too quick, however, for reasons that Alvin Goldman (2007) makes clear:

> As a historical matter, philosophers haven't always described their methodology in the language of intuition. In fact, this seems to be a fairly recent bit of usage. Jaakko Hintikka (1999) traces the philosophical use of "intuition" to Chomsky's description of linguistics' methodology. In the history of philosophy, and even in

the early years of analytic philosophy, the terminology is not to be found . . . This is not to say that historical philosophers and earlier 20th-century philosophers did not make similar philosophical moves. They did make such moves, they just didn't use the term "intuition" to describe them. (p. 2)

The point is this: the fact that philosophers didn't talk *in terms of* intuitions doesn't mean that they weren't talking *about* intuitions, and once we understand what is being said, it becomes clear that intuitions *do* play a central role in these discussions, even if the label doesn't.

Of course, the fact that philosophical intuitions do play a significant role in contemporary philosophy doesn't mean that they either *ought* to play this role, or even that they *need* to play this role. Philosophers don't always have their own methodological best interests in mind. Timothy Williamson (2007) seems to take this view, arguing both that philosophical intuitions are methodologically inessential and that philosophy actually benefits from distancing itself from our philosophical intuitions. Williamson believes that philosophical intuitions are methodologically inessential because he believes that, at least in most cases, we have better evidence. So, for example, our best evidence that knowledge isn't simply justified true belief isn't our philosophical intuition that it is possible for someone to be justified in truly believing that *p* without knowing that *p*, but the *fact* that this is possible. It is the intuitive proposition, and not the fact that the proposition is intuitive, that counts as our best philosophical evidence. Williamson goes even further, arguing not only that we have better evidence than our philosophical intuitions, but also that we have good reason not to treat our philosophical intuitions as evidence, or at least not to limit our philosophical evidence to our philosophical intuitions, namely, that doing so invites philosophical skepticism. By limiting philosophical evidence to our philosophical intuitions we inherit the burden of demonstrating how the fact that it seems to us that some proposition is true provides us with good evidence that it is true; a burden that Williamson thinks it will be impossible to discharge.

In short, Williamson thinks that we can get away with doing philosophy without having to appeal to our philosophical intuitions as evidence and, in fact, that we are much better off doing philosophy in this way since it avoids philosophical skepticism. As I have pointed out elsewhere (Alexander 2010), the problem is that we cannot actually do the kind of philosophical work that we want to do without, in some cases, appealing to our philosophical intuitions. To see why, let's think more about the Gettier cases. According to Williamson, the best evidence we have that knowledge isn't simply justified true belief is the fact that it is possible for someone to have a justified true belief that p without knowing that p. So, for Williamson, something like the following argument is both valid and sound:

(1) Gettier cases are possible (that is, there is nothing inconsistent about the cases).
(2) If a Gettier case were to occur, then the subject would have a justified true belief that p without knowing that p.[13]
(3) Therefore, it is possible for someone to have a justified true belief that p without knowing that p.
(4) Therefore, it is not the case that, necessarily, a person knows that p just in case she has a justified true belief that p.

Since the argument doesn't anywhere mention psychological facts about us, namely, our philosophical intuition that it is possible for someone to have a justified true belief that p without knowing that p, it seems to Williamson that the Gettier cases can work without having to rely on our philosophical intuitions as evidence whatsoever.

But, while it seems to be true that the argument for (4) doesn't require a premise reporting psychological facts about us, namely, our philosophical intuition that it is possible for someone to have a justified true belief that p without knowing that p, that doesn't mean that our philosophical intuitions play no evidentiary role at all in philosophy. Philosophy is, after all, an *argumentative* practice, concerned not only with establishing valid arguments, but also convincing people (sometimes ourselves, sometimes others) that those arguments are sound. And, so not only does the question arise "why should we accept (4)?" – a question whose answer is "because of (1), (2), and (3)"; the question also arises "why should we accept (1), (2), and (3)?" And, here is where our philosophical intuitions seem to play an evidentiary role.

Let's look at premise (2). Why should we accept (2)? Gettier is relying on our philosophical intuitions as evidence that (2) is true. That is, Gettier expects the reader to accept (2) and the basis for this acceptance is its supposed intuitive appeal (to the reader, not just to Gettier).[14] Therefore, intuitions *do* seem to play a role in the argument for (4) – albeit in an indirect way. They don't provide evidence for the truth of (4), itself. But, they do provide evidence for the truth of (at least one) key premise involved in the argument for (4). So, while we may be able to see that the argument is valid without appealing to our philosophical intuitions as evidence, those intuitions do seem to play a role in showing us that the argument is sound. That is, without appealing to our philosophical intuitions, we might be able to see that if (1), (2), and (3) are true, then so is (4) without being able to see that (4) is true.[15]

At this point it might seem like we've missed Williamson's point that our best philosophical evidence consists of known facts about the world. What is our basis for accepting (2)? It would seem that, according to Williamson, our basis for accepting (2) is simply the *fact* that if a Gettier case were to occur, then the subject would have a justified true belief that p without knowing that p.[16] But, can this be right? The argument from the fact that if a Gettier case were to occur, then the subject would have a justified true belief that p without knowing that p to (2) would certainly be valid. After all, the content of (2) just is the claim that if a Gettier case were to occur, then the subject would have a justified true belief that p without knowing that p. And, any proposition validly entails itself. The problem is that such an argument wouldn't have any persuasive force. If a person were not already convinced that a proposition is true, it would hardly help matters to simply assert that, in fact, it is. So, if a person is not already convinced that (2) is true, it hardly helps matters to simply assert that, in fact, if a Gettier case were to occur, then the subject would have a justified true belief that p without knowing that p. As such, the fact that if a Gettier case were to occur, then the subject would have a justified true belief that p without knowing that p simply can't be our *basis* for believing that (2).

If what has been said is right, then it seems as if we must either admit that our best philosophical evidence consists of more than merely known facts about the world or we must abandon the dialectical view of philosophy according to which philosophy is an argumentative practice aimed at rational persuasion and according to which evidence must be capable of helping achieve this aim. Presented with these two options, Williamson seems willing to choose the second and abandon what he calls the "dialectical standard of evidence." According to Williamson, the dialectical standard of evidence opens the door to skepticism.[17] By adopting the view that evidence must be capable of persuading the unpersuaded, and since the skeptic is unpersuaded, we adopt the view that evidence must be capable of persuading the skeptic. But, since the skeptic is not only unpersuaded but unpersuadable, this view leads only to frustration – since the skeptic cannot be persuaded, the dialectical standard of evidence sets a standard that cannot be met. Our only option, according to Williamson, is to reject the goal of persuading the skeptic and, with it, the dialectical standard of evidence. As Williamson writes,

> When one is warranted in refusing to play the skeptic's dialectical game, the dialectical standard of evidence becomes irrelevant. In refusing, one does not abandon one's claims to knowledge and reason, for the appropriate standard of evidence is non-dialectical. By that standard, the skeptic's peremptory challenge fails to disqualify the challenged fact as evidence. To neglect such evidence would be to violate the requirement of total evidence. One continues to assert propositions of the disputed kind on the basis of evidence, without expecting to find arguments for them that use only premises and forms of inference acceptable to the skeptic. Since escape from the radical skeptical predicament is impossible, one must take good care not to get into it in the first place. (2004, p. 123; 2007, p. 239)

It is not clear, however, why we can't adopt a theory of evidence that requires that evidence be capable of persuading the unpersuaded without requiring that evidence be capable of persuading the unpersuadable. Let's distinguish between the following two questions: "what is your reason for believing that p is true?" and "is that a good (enough) reason for believing that p is true?" The goal of the skeptic is to challenge, regardless of what our answer is to the first question, our ability to answer the second question in the affirmative. The skeptic about perception is happy to allow that our reason for believing that p is our perception that p, but casts doubt on the relationship between having the perception that p and p's being true. The skeptic about memory is happy to allow that our reason for believing that p is our memory that p, but casts doubt on the relationship between remembering that p and p's being true. And, the skeptic about judgment is happy to allow that our reason for believing that p is our intuition that p, but casts doubt on the relationship between having the intuition that p and p's being true. The difference, then, between being unpersuaded and being unpersuadable (that is, being skeptical) rests on whether or not a person is willing to accept certain kinds of reasons as good enough reasons for believing that p. A person who is merely unpersuaded about the truth of p is willing to accept that there are reasons that would be good enough for believing that p and is waiting to hear those reasons; a person who is unpersuadable about the truth of p is unwilling to accept that any such reasons exist.[18] But, provided this difference between being unpersuaded and being unpersuadable, there seems to be no good reason for thinking that in order for evidence to be capable of persuading the unpersuaded it must also be capable of persuading the unpersuadable. As such, the fact that nothing will persuade the unpersuadable shouldn't count against a theory of evidence that requires that evidence be capable of persuading the unpersuaded. And, there seems to be no reason why we can't adopt a dialectical theory of evidence that isn't hostage to skeptical worries.

There is also reason to think that we *should* adopt the dialectical theory of evidence. Consider why we value evidence at all. We value evidence because we value justification – that is, we prefer having beliefs that are justified to having beliefs that aren't. Why do we value justification? A natural thought is that we value justification because we value being in a position to be able to defend our beliefs when the truth of those beliefs is called into question. We frequently engage in practices that call upon us to defend our beliefs (either to ourselves or others) – that is, to provide reasons for believing as we do that are capable of persuading the unpersuaded – and we value being able to successfully do so. So, although there is a difference between a person's being justified in believing that p and being able to justify her belief that p, it seems that we value the former, at least in part, because we value the latter. Now, if we value evidence because we value justification, and we value justification at least in part because we value being able to justify our beliefs, what kind of evidence should we value? The obvious answer, it seems, is that we should value evidence that is capable of persuading the unpersuaded – only this kind of evidence will help us to justify our beliefs. As such, it seems that a simple reflection on why we value evidence reveals why we should adopt the dialectical theory of evidence.

Bringing these points together, it seems that we have independent reason to accept a dialectical theory of evidence, namely, the dialectical theory of evidence makes sense of why we value evidence in the first place, and that we can adopt the dialectical theory of evidence without inviting the threat of radical skepticism. If this is right, then given the choice between admitting that evidence in philosophy consists of more than merely known facts about the world or abandoning the dialectical theory of evidence, it seems like we should allow that evidence consists of more than merely known facts about the world. So, where does this leave us? We began by worrying that philosophical intuitions might be philosophically insignificant. Provided the close connection between experimental philosophy and the view that philosophical intuitions are significant, a threat to the significance of our philosophical intuitions is a threat to the significance of experimental philosophy. It turns out, however, that we actually can't do the kind of philosophical work that we want to do without, in some cases, appealing to our philosophical intuitions as evidence that certain philosophical claims are true and as reasons for believing as much, and that appealing to this kind of psychological evidence needn't invite philosophical skepticism.

5. Conclusion

Having canvassed some of the more popular ways of defending the tradition, we can see that there is a common theme to these defenses, namely, the suggestion that experimental philosophers simply haven't been studying the right kind of thing, and that this means that experimental philosophy has little to contribute to our understanding of traditional philosophical practice. But, we've seen that philosophical intuitions play an important role in doing at least some of the work that philosophers want to do, and that attempts to delimit whose intuitions matter or what intuitions matter leave open empirical questions that call for more experimental philosophy rather than less. It is also worth noticing that, since each of these ways of defending the tradition involves something of a departure from some rather common ways of thinking about the tradition, we find ourselves in the somewhat paradoxical position of defending experimental philosophy by defending these ways of thinking about the tradition just so that we can turn right around and challenge those ways of thinking all over again.

Epilogue

1. In Progress . . .

My goal has been to sketch a growing movement, focusing on the relationship between experimental philosophy and the belief that philosophical intuitions provide us with important philosophical insight – that we advance philosophical theories on the basis of their ability to explain our philosophical intuitions, and appeal to them as evidence that those theories are true and as reasons for believing as such. On this way of thinking about philosophy, it makes sense to be interested in studying philosophical cognition, and experimental philosophy has emerged as a fresh approach to studying how people think about philosophical questions, one that makes use of the methods of the social and cognitive sciences. The results have been fascinating, revealing important insights into how our minds work and how we think about philosophical questions. In turn, these insights have raised new concerns about philosophical methodology, and have prompted a return to thinking about what methods we can, and should, employ when doing philosophy. Of course, there is more to be said. There are questions to be answered, details to be secured, and positions to be developed. This is a preliminary study of an ongoing movement, one that has already changed the philosophical landscape, but whose topography is still unfolding.

2. A Note on the Methods of Experimental Philosophy

A great deal of work in experimental philosophy involves the use of survey methods; people are asked to read and respond to philosophical vignettes, and these responses are thought to tell us something important about their philosophical intuitions about what is being said. Recently, concerns have been raised about survey methodology, and it worth spending a moment talking about two of them: one having to do with how people read philosophical vignettes; another having to do with the relationship between survey responses and philosophical intuitions.

Accessibility and Addition

We all understand that the information presented in philosophical vignettes is not always accessible to readers, and that sometimes readers draw on information not presented in the philosophical vignettes themselves when forming judgments about what is being said. Some details are missed; others are added. According to Ernest Sosa (2009), this should give experimental philosophers cause for concern. The methods of experimental philosophy involve asking readers to form judgments about philosophical vignettes; how do we know that these readers are drawing only on the information presented in the philosophical vignettes that they are being asked to consider? Sosa worries that, if we are unable to determine whether readers are responding to the same information, then it is not clear what conclusions we should draw from reports of intuitional disagreement. Perhaps intuitional disagreement is only superficial. If different readers are drawing upon different information, then readers who seem to have different intuitions about the same philosophical vignette might turn out simply to have (appropriately) different intuitions about different philosophical vignettes. Sosa suggests that, unless we can rule this out, we should be concerned about the weight that experimental philosophers have placed on cases of intuitional disagreement when challenging traditional philosophical methodology.

As Joshua Alexander and Jonathan Weinberg (2007) point out, however, there are two problems with this argument. First, the argument rests on an open empirical hypothesis, namely, that different people *systematically* interpret philosophical vignettes differently, and that this plays a significant role in the judgments that they form about what is being said. The only way to substantiate this kind of hypothesis, though, is to engage in careful study of philosophical cognition, and so this argument seems to invite more experimental philosophy, not less. Second, the argument cuts both ways. Whatever problems the argument raises for experimental philosophy, it raises for standard philosophical practice. The argument suggests that, when people talk about specific philosophical vignettes, they can never be sure that they are talking about the same thing. But, if this is true, then not only is it not clear what conclusions we should draw from reports of intuitional disagreement, it is also not clear what conclusions we should draw from reports of intuitional *agreement*. The upshot is a kind of intuitional skepticism that would be as problematic for traditional philosophical methodology as it is for experimental philosophy.

Survey Responses and Philosophical Intuitions

Experimental philosophers ask people to read and respond to philosophical vignettes, but people's responses to questions about philosophical vignettes sometimes reflect not only their judgments about the vignettes themselves, but also sensitivity to conversational context and to specific conversational norms (Schwarz 1995, 1996). According to Simon Cullen (2010), this should worry experimental philosophers, who ask people to read and reflect on philosophical vignettes in strange, and sometimes ambiguous, conversational contexts. Conversational contexts affect how people interpret vignettes and the questions that they are asked about those vignettes, and the more unusual the conversational context the more likely people are to rely on conversational norms to guide their behavior. Cullen believes that this gives us good reason to worry about the relationship between the ways that people respond to questions about philosophical vignettes, what he calls *survey responses*, and their philosophical intuitions.

Cullen is willing to accept that experimental philosophers have shown that survey responses display interesting patterns of diversity and sensitivity. That is, he is willing to accept that different people give different survey responses to questions about particular philosophical vignettes, and that survey responses about particular philosophical vignettes vary according to such things as conversational context. What he wants to argue is that this doesn't give us any reason to think that philosophical intuitions display interesting patterns of diversity and sensitivity. But, it is important to see that a lot depends here on what we think philosophical intuitions are supposed to be. If we think that philosophical intuitions should be insensitive to conversational context or conversational norms, for example, then it makes perfect sense to worry that survey responses aren't telling us something important about our philosophical intuitions. The problem is that Cullen gives us no reason for thinking about philosophical intuitions in this way; he simply adopts a view from Kauppinen (2007), according to which philosophical intuitions are insensitive to pragmatic considerations, and lays out the consequences this view has for the relationship between survey responses and philosophical intuitions. But, having been given no reason for adopting this particular view about philosophical intuitions, we have been given no reason to doubt the relationship between survey responses and philosophical intuitions. There may be other reasons to worry about the relationship between survey responses and philosophical intuitions, but, in the absence of an argument that philosophical intuitions are insensitive to pragmatic considerations, evidence that survey responses are sensitive to pragmatic considerations isn't evidence that they don't reveal important things about our philosophical intuitions.

One last point is worth making here. Although survey methods continue to play a central role in experimental philosophy, the statistical methods and analyses used by experimental philosophers to study the way that people respond to philosophical vignettes have sharpened considerably in recent years (for example, the use of mediation analyses or structural equation modeling). And experimental philosophers have also begun to use a wider array of methods from the social and cognitive sciences: behavioral studies, cognitive load studies, eye-tracking studies, fMRI studies, reaction time studies, and so on. Methodological concerns are sure to arise in the future, as they do with any developing empirical project; but, these should be viewed for what they are, namely, opportunities to improve the empirical methods that we use to study philosophical cognition.

3. Experimental Philosophy as Revolution

Experimental philosophy is sometimes described as a revolution-ary movement – a significant, and maybe even violent, break from more traditional ways of thinking about philosophy. There is a sense in which this characterization is right. Experimental philosophy employs methods more commonly associated with the social and cognitive sciences, has revealed that people think about philosophical questions in quite unexpected ways, and has raised worries about the ways that many of us have come to do philosophy. But it is impor-tant to keep in mind that there is nothing revolutionary about the questions that experimental philosophers ask. They are interested in quite traditional questions about the world and ourselves, about how we think about philosophical questions, and about the methods that we employ when trying to answer them – questions that have shaped Western philosophy from its earliest origins in the Socratic dialogues. It is also important to keep in mind that there is a venerable tradition in philosophy of employing new methods to challenge traditional assumptions about how people think about philosophical questions and how best to pursue answers to those questions. As Richard Rorty (1967) writes, in the very first sentence of his introduction to a collection of some of the most important works of an earlier philo-sophical revolution, "The history of philosophy is punctuated by revolts against the practices of previous philosophers ..." The history of philosophy is the history of revolution; experimental philosophy is simply its latest chapter, a chapter that is still being written.

Notes

Introduction

1. For additional discussion of different ways of dividing up the landscape, see Alexander and Weinberg (2007), Knobe (2007a), Nadelhoffer and Nahmias (2007), Liao (2008), and Alexander et al. (2010a).
2. For additional discussion of this issue, see Nadelhoffer and Nahmias (2007), Knobe (2007a, 2007b), Knobe and Nichols (2008), and Sommers (2011).

Chapter 1 Philosophical Intuitions

1. Bealer (1992, 1996a, 1996b, 1998) and Sosa (1996, 1998) are the most explicit in making this comparison. See, also, Nagel (2007, forthcoming). This way of thinking about things leaves open whether treating intuitions (or perceptions) as evidence involves treating psychological states (or propositions about psychological states) as evidence or treating the *contents* of those psychological states as evidence. As we will see later on, this way of thinking about philosophy isn't shared by all philosophers, even those philosophers who think that intuitions have a role to play in philosophical practice. For example, Kornblith (1998, 2002, 2007) and Williamson (2004, 2005, 2007) argue against the *evidential* role of intuitions while maintaining that they still have some role to play in philosophy, and Gendler (2007) has recently argued that the role of philosophical thought experiments is not to generate intuitions

that can be used as evidence for, or against, philosophical claims, but to help make philosophical theories cognitively accessible.

2. Some philosophers take these theories to be telling us something about the psychological world (that is, about our individual or shared psychological concepts of things), while others take these claims to be telling us something about the non-psychological world (that is, about things themselves, platonic forms, Fregean concepts, etc.). For discussion, see Goldman and Pust (1998) and Goldman (2007). We will set aside this distinction for the time being before picking it up again in the next chapter.

3. This is not to say that *everyone* changed his or her mind. Weatherson (2003), for example, argues that our reasons for believing that knowledge is justified true belief trump the evidence provided by the philosophical intuitions generated in response to Gettier's two hypothetical cases.

4. It is important to keep in mind that when philosophers appeal to intuitions as evidence, they are not (at least typically) appealing merely to their own intuitions. Philosophical analysis is not mere intellectual autobiography and for good reason: an appeal to one's own intuitions would not be dialectically effective. For further discussion, see Alexander and Weinberg (2007).

5. Descriptivism has seen a revival in recent years associated with the rise of two-dimensional semantics. See, e.g., Chalmers (1996), Jackson (1998a, 1998b), and Stalnaker (1999).

6. For additional discussion of the doctrine of double effect and various versions of the trolley case, including versions of the trolley case that are thought to generate intuitional evidence inconsistent with the doctrine of double effect, see Foot (1967), Thomson (1985), Kamm (1989, 2007), and Liao et al. (forthcoming).

7. The first strategy has been endorsed by Lynch (2006), the second strategy by Bealer (1998), Sosa (1998), and Pust (2000), and the third strategy by Williamson (2007). Although we won't press this point here, the third strategy is probably the best. One problem with the first strategy is that it isn't clear that we have *any* intuitions about what intuitions are (or, at least, whether or not intuitions are the sort of thing about which we have intuitions will depend on just what intuitions turn out to be) and so the strategy is unlikely to provide much help to us in determining which conception is correct. And, one problem with the second strategy is that there is little consensus about what intuitions are like amongst those philosophers who appeal to what intuitions seem like from a first-person perspective and so this strategy is just as likely to cause confusion as to clear it up. The third strategy avoids the thorny

question of whether or not philosophical intuitions are the kinds of things about which we have intuitions and the confusion that results from the varied first-person, introspective accounts of what intuitions seem to us to be. It also has the advantage of theoretical conservatism by not building anything more into an account of philosophical intuitions than that which is minimally necessary in order to capture their role in philosophical practice.

8. Of course, this doesn't mean that all beliefs or inclinations to believe are philosophical intuitions; almost all philosophers want to put some restriction on what kinds of beliefs or inclinations to believe could count as philosophical intuitions; for example, most philosophers argue that philosophical intuitions should be *immediate* or at least *not explicitly inferential*. It is also worth pointing out here that, while the philosophers mentioned in the section typically remain neutral about whether philosophical intuitions are beliefs or inclinations to believe, others, who endorse some kind of doxastic approach, are more partisan on this matter. So, for example, Sosa (1998) and Earlenbaugh and Molyneux (2009a, 2009b) have advanced conceptions that treat philosophical intuitions specifically as inclinations or dispositions to believe.

9. It is probably worth noting here that Williamson actually suggests that the practice of appealing to philosophical intuitions as evidence rests on a misunderstanding of the nature of philosophical evidence, arguing that philosophers "might be better off not using the word 'intuition' and its cognates" since our emphasis on intuitional evidence doesn't help "to answer questions about the nature of evidence on offer but to fudge them, by appearing to provide answers without really doing so" (2007, p. 220). We will discuss Williamson's argument against the philosophical significance of philosophical intuitions in Chapter 5. See, also, Alexander (2010).

10. For additional discussion of this point, see Weinberg and Alexander (forthcoming).

11. Bealer defends this view over a number of papers. See, also, Bealer (1992, 1996a, 1996b). The view that philosophical intuitions present their propositional contents as necessary has also been defended by BonJour (1992, 1998), Plantinga (1993), Sosa (1996), and Hales (2000). Sosa (2007b), Talbot (2009), and Bengson (forthcoming) have recently advanced phenomenological conceptions that don't involve the claim that philosophical intuitions present their propositional contents as necessary, instead saying only that genuine philosophical intuitions are "conscious states of felt attraction", "strike us as true without us knowing entirely why they do", or "strike us in a certain way", respectively.

12. Bealer (1998) provides two other reasons for thinking that intuitions are not beliefs. First, he argues that beliefs are plastic in a way that intuitions are not; while you can get someone to believe almost anything at all, it seems to be impossible to get certain propositions to seem to be true in the relevant phenomenological sense of "seems". Second, he argues that there are no significant limitations to the kinds of propositions about which you can have beliefs while there are limitations to the kinds of propositions about which you can have intuitions. We will focus on Bealer's first two reasons because they seem to be, on balance, stronger reasons for maintaining that philosophical intuitions are not beliefs. First, it is neither clear that *all* beliefs are plastic (consider, for example, your belief that you currently exist) nor clear that sufficient psychological stress or torture couldn't make anything at all seem to be true to you in the relevant phenomenological sense of "seems". Second, even if it were true that there are propositions about which you can have beliefs but not intuitions, this wouldn't necessarily show that intuitions aren't beliefs – it might only show that intuitions are a subclass of beliefs.

13. Another point of controversy has been the claim that philosophical intuitions are *sui generis* propositional attitudes. Both Sosa (1998) and Williamson (2007), for example, argue that they find no intellectual seeming that *p* beyond their own conscious inclinations to believe that *p*.

14. Ludwig (2010) argues that the semantic approach is also too liberal, letting in certain things that we don't want to count as philosophical intuitions. As Ludwig points out, some abstract propositions – for example, the claim that there is no greatest prime number – are simply too complicated for us to form intuitions about them.

15. For additional discussion of this issue, see Kornblith (2002), Weinberg and Alexander (forthcoming), and Weinberg et al. (forthcoming).

Chapter 2 Experimental Philosophy and Philosophical Analysis

1. See, for example, Strawson (1986), Kane (1999), O'Connor (2000), Pereboom (2001), and Pink (2004).

2. More specifically, 72% of subjects who were asked to evaluate Jeremy's actions in the *Supercomputer* case judged that he acted of his own free will when he robbed the bank, while 83% of subjects judged that he was morally *blameworthy* for his actions. Interestingly, it doesn't appear that subjects were influenced by the negative nature of Jeremy's actions. When subjects were asked to consider a similar vignette in which Jeremy saved the life of a child, 68% of subjects judged that he

acted of his own free will while 88% of subjects judged that he was morally *praiseworthy* for his actions. In order to make sure that causal determinism was sufficiently salient, Nahmias et al. considered two additional vignettes: one in which a universe is re-created over and over again with the same initial conditions and laws of nature, another in which the people's actions are completely determined by genetic and environmental factors. In both cases, most subjects who were asked to evaluate an agent's actions in the cases judged that the agent acted of his (her) own free will even though those actions were causally determined and judged that the agent was morally responsible for his (her) actions.

3. A quick note about how determinism is described in these studies. Nahmias et al. (2007) suggest that people's philosophical intuitions are also influenced by how determinism is described. In particular, they found that people are more likely to express compatibilist intuitions when determinism is described in nonmechanistic, psychological terms than when determinism is described in mechanistic, neuroscientific terms. Interestingly, they still found that people's emotional responses to affectively charged vignettes influence their intuitive judgments about whether moral responsibility is compatible with causal determinism, regardless of how determinism is described. Roskies and Nichols (2008) also found that people's philosophical intuitions are influenced by how determinism is described. They found that people's philosophical intuitions are sensitive to whether deterministic scenarios are presented as actual or merely possible.

4. More specifically, 86% of subjects who were asked whether it is possible in Universe A for an agent to be fully morally responsible for her actions judged that it is not possible.

5. More specifically, 72% of subjects who were asked to consider the *Murderous Husband* case judged that Bill was morally responsible for his actions.

6. In order to rule out the possibility that people's judgments are tracking abstractness/concreteness alone, Nichols and Knobe ran a second study involving only high affect (involving habitual rape) and low affect (involving habitual tax evasion) concrete cases. Their results confirmed that people are more likely to say that a person is morally responsible for her actions in high affect cases than in low affect cases even when her actions are causally determined.

7. For further discussion of this point, see Alexander et al. (2010a, 2010b).

8. Marr (1982) calls this the *computational* level, Pylyshyn (1984) calls this the *semantic* level, and Glass et al. (1979) call this the *content* level.

9. Marr (1982) calls these two levels the *algorithmic* and *implementational*

levels, Pylyshyn (1984) calls them the *syntactic* and *physical* levels, and Glass et al. (1979) call them the *form* and *medium* levels.

10. More specifically, 67% of subjects who were asked to consider both cases judged that neither Bill nor Mark is morally responsible for his actions, 25% of subjects who were asked to consider both cases judged that both Bill and Mark are morally responsible for their actions, and 8% of subjects who were asked to consider both cases gave mixed answers.

11. For additional discussion of this dilemma, see Alexander et al. (2010a).

12. See, e.g., Christensen (2007), Elga (2006), Feldman (2006), Feldman and Warfield (2007), Kelly (2005, 2007, 2008), and White (2005).

13. For recent discussions of relativism, see Boghossian (2006) and Hales (2006).

14. Although, recent work by Nahmias and Murray (2011) presents interesting evidence that might provide the basis for discounting one set of philosophical intuitions about moral responsibility. They found that most people who think that freedom and moral responsibility are incompatible with causal determinism do so because they mistakenly believe that causal determinism involves some kind of *fatalism* when agent's mental states (including intentions) are bypassed in the relevant causal processes.

15. Sommers (2010) provides a number of suggestions about how to address some of the worries discussed above, and points to a number of questions worth addressing as experimental research on this topic moves forward.

16. For other vignettes commonly appealed to in this debate, see Cohen (1998), Fantl and McGrath (2002), and Stanley (2005).

17. See, for example, DeRose (1992), Lewis (1996), and Cohen (1998).

18. See, for example, Fantl and McGrath (2002), Hawthorne (2004), and Stanley (2005). Stanley calls his brand of invariantism *interest-relevant invariantism*.

19. Actually, the debate between contextualists and subject-sensitive invariantists is a bit more complicated since both groups agree that knowledge is sensitive to what is at stake for the subject. What they disagree about is whether or not making salient the possibility that the subject is wrong affects epistemic standards. Contextualists think that it does; invariants think that it does not. As such, the debate isn't really about whether salience matters or stakes matter (since both sides accept that stakes do matter) but about whether or not salience matters.

20. More specifically, subjects were asked to rate (using a 5-point Likert scale with 1 = strongly disagree and 5 = strongly agree) the degree to which they agreed or disagreed that Bruno knows that the bank will be

open on Saturday. The mean response for subjects who were asked to consider the *Low Standards Bank* case was 3.83, while the mean response for subjects who were asked to consider the *High Standards Bank* case was 3.64.

21. More specifically, subjects were asked to rate (using a 7-point Likert scale with 1 = strongly disagree and 7 = strongly agree) the degree to which they agreed or disagreed that Hannah knows that the bank will be open on Saturday. The mean response for subjects who were asked to consider the *Low Stakes No Alternative* case was 5.07, while the mean response for subjects who were asked to consider the *High Stakes Alternative* case was 4.60.

22. DeRose (2011) has raised several concerns about these studies, including that participants in some studies are asked to rate their willingness to *make* knowledge attributions rather than being asked to *evaluate* knowledge attributions, and that when participants are asked to evaluate knowledge attributions, they are asked to do so even in situations where it would be more natural to deny knowledge. Since what conversational context is relevant depends (at least in part) on whether you are being asked to make a knowledge attribution or to evaluate a knowledge attribution, and since being asked to evaluate knowledge attributions when it is natural to deny knowledge introduces a host of pragmatic implications that can influence our judgments, DeRose is worried that these studies fail to actually test the truth or plausibility of epistemic contextualism. While these are legitimate concerns, Buckwalter (forthcoming) finds that salience doesn't seem to matter even when these concerns have been addressed in the experimental design of the studies. DeRose also raises a host of more general concerns about the methods employed by experimental philosophers; these concerns will be addressed in the epilogue.

23. See, also, Fantl and McGrath (2002) and Hawthorne (2004).

24. More specifically, subjects were asked to rate (using a 7-point Likert scale with 1 = strongly agree and 7 = strongly disagree) the degree to which they agreed or disagreed that Hannah knows that the bank will be open on Saturday. The mean response for subjects who were asked to consider the *Simplified Low Stakes* case was 3.85, while the mean response for subjects who were asked to consider the *Simplified High Stakes* case was 3.83. Feltz and Zarpentine (2010) also found no statistically significant differences in people's intuitive judgments about analogous high and low stakes cases. Actually, when they collapsed all of the high stakes and low stakes experiments they ran, they did find a statistically significant difference, but the effect size barely escaped triviality. This should be little solace, then, for those philosophers who

think that stakes are an important and pervasive influence on knowledge attributions.

25. More specifically, subjects were asked to rate (using a 7-point Likert scale with 1 = not confident and 7 = very confident) how confident Kate should be that she is on Main Street. The mean response for subjects who were asked to consider the *Unimportant* case was 5.11, while the mean response for subjects who were asked to consider the *Important* case was 4.93.

26. Although, Brown (forthcoming) has recently argued that the insensitivity of folk knowledge attributions to things like stakes and salience undermines contextualism but not subject-sensitive invariantism.

27. More specifically, subjects were asked to rate (using a 7-point Likert scale with 1 = disagree and 7 = agree) the degree to which they agreed or disagreed that Hannah knows that the bank will be open on Saturday. The mean response for subjects who were asked to consider the *Revised Low Standard* case was 5.54, while the mean response for subjects who were asked to consider the *Concrete High Standard* case was 3.05. This difference was statistically significant at the level $p < 0.001$. Nagel (2010) also found that salience matters, finding that making error possibilities salient makes people less likely to agree with knowledge assertions and more likely to agree with knowledge denials.

28. More specifically, the median response for subjects asked to consider the *Low Stakes Typo* case was 2 and the median response for subjects asked to consider the *High Stakes Typo* case was 5. This difference was statistically significant at the level $p < 0.001$.

29. Pinillos and Simpson (forthcoming) respond to this worry with a series of new studies that focus more directly on knowledge attributions and that still find evidence that stakes matter.

30. See Hawthorne and Stanley (2008) for an interesting discussion of the relationship between knowledge and rational action.

31. Weatherson (forthcoming) argues that what might seem like inconclusive evidence that stakes matter is actually conclusive evidence after all. According to Weatherson, subject-sensitive invariantists don't think that stakes *always* matter; instead, they simply think that stakes *sometimes* matter. If this is right, then we should be less concerned by the fact that some experimental studies showed that stakes matter while others don't.

Chapter 3 Experimental Philosophy and the Philosophy of Mind

1. See also Goldman and Pust (1998). Goldman's worry is similar to what has come to be known as *Benacerraf's Problem*: according to our best

theory of mathematical truth, mathematical statements refer to abstract entities; but, according to our best theory of knowledge, a person knows that *p* only if there is a causal connection between that person and whatever it is that makes *p* true; since abstract entities cannot stand in causal relationships, there is a problem. This worry leads Goldman to endorse *mentalism*, the view that philosophical intuitions are evidence only about certain facts (the structure or meaning, for example) of our concepts.

2. More specifically, 82% of subjects who were asked to evaluate the chairman's actions in the *Environmental Harm* case judged that the chairman intentionally harmed the environment, while only 23% of subjects who were asked to evaluate the chairman's actions in the *Environmental Help* case judged that the chairman intentionally helped the environment. This difference is statistically significant at the level $p < 0.001$. Knobe (2003a) found that similar results obtain for a different pair of vignettes with the same basic structure.

3. More specifically, 76% of subjects who were asked to evaluate Jake's actions in the *No Skill/Immoral Outcome* case judged that he hit his aunt intentionally, while only 28% of subjects who were asked to evaluate Jake's actions in the *No Skill/Positive Outcome* case judged that he hit the bull's-eye intentionally. This difference is statistically significant at the level $p < 0.01$. In addition to the two studies discussed, Cushman and Mele (2008), Knobe (2004a, 2004b), Knobe and Burra (2006), Knobe and Mendlow (2004), Leslie et al. (2006), Malle (2006), McCann (2005), Mele and Cushman (2007), Nadelhoffer (2004a, 2004b, 2005, 2006a, 2006b), and Young et al. (2006) have found that similar results obtain for different pairs of vignettes with the same basic structure.

4. Recently, a third explanation has come into fashion; namely, that these results tell us something about the relationship between moral judgments and *folk psychology* more generally, and is best explained in terms of specific features of the underlying mechanism responsible for a broad range of folk psychological judgments. See, e.g., Knobe (2006), Nadelhoffer (2006b), Alicke (2008), Nado (2008), and Pettit and Knobe (2009).

5. Grice (1989) introduced the notion of conversational implicature to refer to something that is suggested by a sentence when this is distinct from what is expressed or entailed by the literal meaning of the sentence.

6. A similar story can be provided to explain why people tend to say that the chairman helped the environment unintentionally. People do not want to praise the chairman for helping the environment in

the *Environmental Help* case. If they said that the chairman helped the environment intentionally, then this would imply that he should be praised for his actions. As a result, when they are asked whether or not the chairman helped the environment intentionally, people tend to say that the chairman didn't help the environment intentionally. Again, people's tendency to say that the chairman didn't help the environment intentionally doesn't reflect the nature of their folk concept of *intentional action*; it merely reflects their desire to refrain from praising the chairman for helping the environment.

7. More specifically, using a rating scale ranging from -3 ('sounds wrong') to $+3$ ('sounds right'), people who were asked to consider the *Environmental Harm* case were asked whether or not it sounded right to say that the chairman harmed the environment in order to increase profits and those who were asked to consider the *Environmental Help* case were asked whether or not it sounded right to say that the chairman helped the environment in order to increase profits. The average rating for people who were asked to consider the *Environmental Harm* case was $+0.6$ and the average rating for people who were asked to consider the *Environmental Help* case was -1.0. This difference is statistically significant at the level $p = 0.01$.

8. Malle (2006) offers a number of his own interpretations of the results. Among the most interesting interpretations is that the side-effect effect might best be interpreted as resulting from the way in which the vignettes are presented. According to Malle, since participants' attention is focused on the evaluative components of the vignette, they might think that they are supposed to use their moral evaluations when making their intentionality judgments. In other contexts where their attention isn't so focused, they might not let their evaluative judgments drive their intentionality judgments.

9. Knobe (2003b) draws this case from Mele (2001).

10. Malle and Nelson (2003) also argue that these results are best explained in terms of affective bias. They studied couples engaged in heated arguments (arguments in which each party develops a sufficiently negative affective response to the other party) and found that such couples typically judge all of their opponent's actions as intentional – even those that would not otherwise be so judged. These studies suggest to them that negative affective responses *distort* people's intentionality judgments.

11. Nadelhoffer (2004a) argues that positive affective responses seem to have a similar influence on people's intentionality judgments. Consider the following vignette:

Academic Help:
Imagine that Steve and Jason are two friends who are competing against one another in an essay competition. Jason decides to help Steve edit his essay. Ellen, a mutual friend, says, "Don't you realize that if you help Steve, you will decrease your own chances of winning the competition?" Jason responds, "I know that helping Steve decreases my chances of winning, but I don't care at all about that. I just want to help my friend!" Sure enough, Steve wins the competition because of Jason's help.

Nadelhoffer found that most people who were asked to consider the *Academic Help* case have a positive affective response to Jason and judge that Jason decreased his own chances of winning the competition intentionally.

12. More specifically, using a rating scale ranging from 0 (no blame) to 6 (lots of blame), people who were asked to consider the *Police Officer* case were asked how much blame the thief deserved for the death of the officer and those who were asked to consider the *Car Thief* case were asked how much blame the driver deserved for the death of the thief. The average rating for people who were asked to consider the *Police Officer* case was 5.11 and the average rating for people who were asked to consider the *Car Thief* case was 2.01. Nadelhoffer associates people's negative affective responses with their willingness to ascribe blame and concludes that people asked to consider the *Police Officer* case had a stronger negative affective response than those asked to consider the *Car Thief* case.

13. More specifically, 37% of subjects who were asked to consider the *Police Officer* case judged that the thief intentionally brought about the officer's death, while only 10% of subjects who were asked to consider the *Car Thief* case judged that the driver intentionally brought about the car thief's death. This result is statistically significant at the level $p <$ 0.001.

14. Knobe and Mendlow (2004) argue that evidence also suggests that people are willing to withhold blame in cases where a morally bad outcome is thought to be intentional.

15. In fact, Guglielmo and Malle (2010) argue that evidence suggests that people often blame the chairman for harming the environment *because* they believe that the chairman did so intentionally.

16. This might be too strong. It is possible that a number of different factors might play a role in generating our intentionality judgments, and that blame and affect might *sometimes* be among these factors. What the considerations just rehearsed do is put pressure on the idea that these things are the only factors responsible for our intentionality judgments.

17. For additional discussion, see Alexander et al. (2010a, 2010b).

18. Phelan and Sarkissian (2009) argue that there are two problems with the *Extra Dollar* case. First, if people view paying an extra dollar for a smoothie as a cost, they are likely to view it is a bad thing (although maybe not morally bad). As such, the case doesn't seem to be right for deciding between an explanation of the side-effect effect according to which people's intuitions about whether or not an action was performed intentionally are being influenced by normative considerations and an explanation of the side-effect effect according to which people's intuitions about whether or not an action was performed intentionally are being influenced simply by considerations of costs and benefits. (Phelan and Sarkissian have a similar worry about the subject-oriented reading of the trade-off hypothesis discussed below; namely, that it comes close to Knobe's own hypothesis that people's intuitions about whether or not an action was performed intentionally are being influenced by normative considerations.) Second, it is not clear that the *Extra Dollar* case actually involves a foreseen side effect. Recall that an outcome is a foreseen side effect just in case an agent chooses to perform an action that she foresees will bring about the outcome but doesn't perform the action for the purpose of trying to bring it about. But, something done in order to bring about a specific outcome isn't a side effect of an action performed to bring about that outcome; it is part of the action performed in order to bring it about. As such, since the agent pays an extra dollar in order to get the Mega-Sized Smoothie, paying the extra dollar isn't a side effect at all.

19. More specifically, 95% of subjects who were asked to evaluate Joe's actions in the *Extra Dollar* case judged that he intentionally paid an extra dollar, while only 45% of subjects who were asked to evaluate Joe's actions in the *Free Cup* case judged that he intentionally bought the commemorative cup. This difference is statistically significant at the level $p < 0.001$.

20. More specifically, 56% of subjects who were asked to evaluate John's actions in the *Worker* case judged that he intentionally caused the death of the workman on the side tracks, while only 23% of subjects who were asked to consider the *Dog* case judged that John intentionally saved the dog. This difference is statistically significant at the level $p < 0.01$.

21. Phelan and Sarkissian (2009) point out that there is a problem with using this study to challenge Knobe's hypothesis. While most people view both actions as morally appropriate, Phelan and Sarkissian speculate that most people would think that the first action (causing the death of the workman on the side track) is bad (although maybe not *morally*

bad), while the second action (saving the dog) is good (probably even morally good). If this is right, then Knobe's hypothesis would actually predict these results.

22. See Mallon (2009) and Phelan and Sarkissian (2009).

23. More specifically, 92% of subjects who were asked to evaluate the terrorist's action in the *Harmful Terrorist* case judged that the terrorist intentionally harmed the Australians, while only 12% of subjects who were asked to evaluate the terrorist's action in the *Helpful Terrorist* case judged that the terrorist intentionally helped the orphanage. This difference is statistically significant at the level $p < 0.0001$. Mallon (2009) based these vignettes on vignettes introduced by Knobe and Kelly (2009). Mallon found that similar results obtain for a different pair of vignettes with the same basic structure.

24. Since the vignette specifies that the lieutenant also views the soldiers' deaths as a cost, this result provides additional evidence against the view that people's intuitions about whether or not an action was performed intentionally are being influenced by the fictional agent's perception of something as a cost.

25. Phelan and Sarkissian (2009) have another argument against the subject-oriented reading. According to them, if the subject-oriented reading is correct, then we should expect people to be more willing to judge that an action is intentional when they perceive it as a cost incurred in the pursuit of an important goal than when they perceive it as a cost incurred in the pursuit of an unimportant goal. Since they find experimental evidence to suggest that this is not the case, they conclude that the subject-oriented reading is incorrect. The problem is that there is no reason, on any version of the trade-off hypothesis, to expect people to be more willing to judge that an action is intentional when they perceive it as a cost incurred in the pursuit of an important goal than when they perceive it as a cost incurred in the pursuit of an unimportant goal. Costs are costs. For the trade-off hypothesis, nothing hinges on whether the agent was wise to incur the costs. All that matters is that costs incurred are incurred intentionally.

Chapter 4 Experimental Philosophy and Philosophical Methodology

1. For wonderful discussions of other forms of cultural cognitive diversity, see Nisbett et al. (2001), Nisbett and Norenzayan (2002), and Nisbett (2003). Nisbett and colleagues have found that a variety of different cognitive processes, including perception and memory, display cultural sensitivity. For an early, and influential, study of moral intuitions and cultural diversity, see Haidt et al. (1993).

2. In particular, they found that 26% of Western subjects, 56% of East Asian subjects, and 61% of South Asian subjects judged that Bob knows that Jill drives an American car. The difference between Western subjects and both East Asian and South Asian subjects is statistically significant at the level $p < 0.01$.

3. In particular, descriptivist judgments about the vignettes received a score of 0 while causal-historical judgments received a score of 1. The scores for each vignette were then summed so that the cumulative score could range from 0 to 2. Using this procedure, Machery and his colleagues found that Western subjects were more likely than East Asian subjects to have causal-historical intuitions. The difference between the mean response for Western subjects (1.13) and the mean response for East Asian subjects (0.63) is statistically significant at the level $p < 0.05$. For recent discussions of this study, including both theoretical and empirical concerns, see Ludwig (2007), Deutsch (2009), Marti (2009), Sytsma and Livengood (2011), and Ichikawa et al. (forthcoming).

4. A close look at the empirical results might suggest that this move is rather unique even *within* Western culture since even a significant amount of people from Western backgrounds have intuitions about these cases that are inconsistent with the causal-historical account of reference.

5. More specifically, subjects were asked to rate (using a 7-point Likert scale with 1 = strongly disagree and 7 = strongly agree) the degree to which they agreed or disagreed that it is morally acceptable to redirect the trolley in the two cases. In the *Stranger* case, the mean response for men was 4.21, while the mean response for women was 4.95. In the *Child* case, the mean response for women was 4.26, while the mean response for men was 4.87. The difference between responses by men and women to these two cases approached statistical significance with $p = 0.07$. In addition to these two cases, Zamzow and Nichols asked subjects to consider cases in which the individual on the side track was the participant's brother and cases in which the individual on the side track was the participant's sister. Interestingly, they found that men judged killing one's brother to be less morally acceptable than women ($M = 3.41$ vs. $M = 4.33$) and that women judged killing one's sister to be less morally acceptable than men ($M = 3.78$ vs. $M = 4.40$). As Zamzow and Nichols write, "there appears to be a bias in favor of one's own gender, at least when it comes to siblings and speeding trains."

6. More specifically, only 41% of male subjects said that Peter "really knows" that there is a watch on the table, while 71% of female participants said that Peter "really knows" that there is a watch on the table. This difference is statistically significant at the level $p < 0.05$. In order

to rule out the possibility that the effect was being driven by the gender of the protagonist, Starmans and Friedman ran another study using a slightly different vignette whose protagonist was female. If anything, the results were even more striking. In this version, only 36% of male participants said that the female protagonist really knows, while 75% of female participants said that she really knows. This difference is statistically significant at the level $p < 0.01$.

7. More specifically, only 35% of male participants said that someone in this world could be free to choose whether or not to murder someone else, while 63% of female participants said that someone in this world could be free to choose whether or not to murder someone else. This difference is statistically significant at the level $p < 0.0005$.

8. In fact, there is some evidence that interpersonal intuitional diversity is even finer grained than this, tracking individual personality types. See, e.g., Cokely and Feltz (2009) and Feltz and Cokely (2007, 2009).

9. Zamzow and Nichols (2009) provide a different reason to think that we should not worry so much about intuitional diversity. Drawing on the analogy between intuitional evidence and empirical evidence, they argue that lessons from the history of science, together with work from the social and cognitive sciences, indicate that evidential diversity is actually an epistemic good to be promoted rather than feared. The idea is that evidential diversity plays a role in epistemic progress. Zamzow and Nichols are certainly right that more attention should be paid to the epistemic benefits of evidential diversity, but for our purposes, it's important to keep in mind that change involves choice – the resolution or at least dissolution of disagreements – and that any claim to progress requires some way of defending those choices as right. It is not clear, then, that their suggestion takes us past the need for a principled way of resolving evidential diversity, although it might make us more sanguine about our prospects for being able to find one.

10. Moral intuitions also seem to be sensitive to facts about the person who is considering the hypothetical case. Zamzow and Nichols (2009) recently found that moral intuitions demonstrate sensitivity to gender.

11. Uhlmann et al. (2009) used a linear regression to test for independent and interactive effects between scenario condition (Tyrone Payton vs. New York Philharmonic $= -1$/Chip Ellsworth III vs. Harlem Jazz Orchestra $= 1$), political orientation (1 = very liberal, 5 = very conservative) and endorsement of consequentialism (1 = completely disagree, 7 = completely agree). They found a reliable lower-order effect: subjects were less willing to endorse consequentialism when Tyrone Payton was sacrificed than they were when Chip Ellsworth III was sacrificed ($b = -0.19$, $SE = 0.09$, $t(84) = 2.24$, $p = 0.03$). The effect was even more

pronounced for people who self-identified as politically liberal (1 SD below the mean): $b = -0.40$, $SE = 0.12$, $t = 3.27$, $p = 0.002$.

12. Those who identify themselves as politically conservative aren't immune from this kind of intuitional sensitivity. In a separate study, Uhlmann and his colleagues found that people who identified themselves as politically conservative were more likely to think that it is morally permissible for American military forces to engage in an action that involved collateral civilian casualties to stop Iraqi insurgents than they were to think that it is morally permissible for Iraqi insurgents to engage in an action that involved collateral civilian casualties to stop American military forces.

13. More specifically, subjects were asked to rate (using a 5-point Likert scale with 1 = strongly disagree and 5 = strongly agree) the degree to which they agreed or disagreed that Charles knows that it is 71 degrees in the room. The mean response for subjects who were asked to evaluate the *Truetemp* case before evaluating any other cases was 2.8; the mean response for subjects who were asked to evaluate the *Truetemp* case after first being asked to evaluate a clear case of knowledge was 2.4; and the mean response for subjects who were asked to evaluate the *Truetemp* case after first being asked to evaluate a clear case of non-knowledge was 3.2. The difference between these conditions is statistically significant at the level $p < 0.05$. These results were confirmed, replicated, and extended by Wright (2010), who offers an interesting explanation of intuitional sensitivity to presentation order, and by Weinberg et al. (forthcoming), who examined the relationship between people's *need-for-cognition* (Cacioppo and Petty 1982) and intuitional sensitivity to presentation order.

14. For a fascinating discussion of this work, together with a discussion of the methodological problems that this kind of sensitivity raises for traditional philosophical methodology, see Sinnott-Armstrong (2008).

15. Subjects were asked to indicate their willingness to act to save the five track workers using a scale ranging from +5 to −5. The mean when the switch version appeared first was 3.1, the mean when the switch version appeared third was 1.0. The mean when the fat-man version appeared first was −0.86, the mean when the fat-man version appeared third was −1.7. These results are significant at the level $p < 0.005$.

16. As before, subjects were asked to indicate their willingness to act to save the five track workers using a scale ranging from +5 to −5. The mean response when the button version followed the switch version was 2.7; the mean response when the button version followed the fat-man version was 0.65. This result is significant at the level $p < 0.02$.

17. The Petrinovich and O'Neill study is somewhat limited by the fact that they asked what people *would do* rather than what people thought was *morally permissible* or *morally right*. As Zamzow and Nichols (2009) rightly note, "judgments of what you would do in a situation can come apart from your moral judgments". This problem has been resolved in more recent studies on the contextual sensitivity of moral intuitions (and, in particular, *Trolley* intuitions). See, in particular, Liao et al. (forthcoming) and Schwitzgebel and Cushman (2011).

18. In fact, there are at least two extant philosophical theories according to which some of these things – in particular, cultural background and context – *are* relevant: namely, relativism and contextualism. According to relativism, the truth or falsity of certain philosophical claims depends – at least, in part – on facts about the person evaluating the claim. And, according to contextualism, the truth or falsity of certain philosophical claims depends – at least, in part – on the context in which those claims are made and evaluated. (For recent discussions of relativism, see Boghossian 2006 and Hales 2006, and for recent discussions of contextualism, see DeRose 1995, Lewis 1996, and Cohen 1998.) While it is somewhat beyond the scope of the present work to evaluate how successful either theory might be at explaining why such things as cultural background, gender, affective content, or context might be relevant to the truth or falsity of philosophical claims, two points are worth considering. First, what has been shown by these studies is that some philosophical intuitions *are* sensitive to cultural background, gender, affectivity, and context. What the relativist or contextualist needs, however, is some independent argument that philosophical intuitions *should* be sensitive to these kinds of things. That is, they need some way to move from the descriptive claim to the normative claim. Second, it is not clear that relativism or contextualism – taken individually or jointly – can explain why *all* of the things are relevant.

Chapter 5 In Defense of Experimental Philosophy

1. This label comes from Weinberg et al. (2010), who provide the first detailed discussion of the strengths and weaknesses of this defense. Singer (1972, 1982), Devitt (1994, 2006, 2010), Williamson (2005, 2007), Hales (2006), Ludwig (2007), Grundmann (2010), and Horvath (2010) advance versions of the expertise defense. Interestingly, its central tenet (that philosophers should be more concerned with the intuitions of experts than those of the folk) can also be found in Stich and Nisbett's (1980) discussion of the method of reflective equilibrium and the justification of rules of inference. Concerned that a significant

number of unacceptable rules of inference stand in reflective equilibrium with folk inferential practices, they argue that a rule of inference is justified just in case it stands in reflective equilibrium to the inferential practices of trained authorities, or experts. It is important to note, however, that Stich (1988) takes back this earlier defense of expert reflective equilibrium.

2. Jackman (2001), Nichols (2004a), Goldman (2007), and Knobe and Nichols (2008) make similar points.

3. Ludwig (2007) makes this suggestion, writing about expertise that it "is not a matter of acquiring new concepts! It is a matter of gaining greater sensitivity to the structure of the concepts through reflective exercise with problems involving those concepts" (p. 149).

4. Ludwig (2007) seems to have something similar in mind in the following example: Mr. Smith, a normal fit man in his twenties, is standing by the window in his living room. He hears the phone ring on the side table by the couch on the other side of the room. He walks to the side table across the open floor between him and the phone and picks it up. Which of the following is true: (A) Mr. Smith tried to walk across the living room; (B) Mr. Smith did not try to walk across the living room; or (C) Neither (A) nor (B). According to Ludwig, we *see* that (A) is the correct answer since this answer best fits our best theory of intentional action, according to which a person can attempt to do something even in cases in which it is almost assured that he will succeed.

5. See Livengood et al. (2010) for an interesting empirical study that suggests that philosophers are more reflective than the folk.

6. Kornblith (2002) provides two nice examples. Kornblith's first example is Nisbett and Wilson's (1977) study on position effects. Nisbett and Wilson found that people's assessment of consumer goods is influenced by the relative position of the goods being evaluated. Even when asked to reflect on what factors contributed to their assessment, people remain unaware of the influence of relative position on their assessments. Kornblith's second example is Tversky and Kahneman's (1974) study on anchoring effects. In this study, subjects were asked to estimate the percentage of African nations that are members of the United Nations. When asked if the percentage was greater or less than 10%, the mean estimate was 25%; when asked if the percentage was greater or less than 65%, the mean estimate was 45%. While it is clear that subjects are influenced by the initial reference point (the "anchor"), subjects are completely unaware of the influence that this reference point has on their estimates.

7. In fact, Weinberg et al. (forthcoming) give us reason to worry that even reflective intuitions display the same kinds of problematic intuitional

sensitivities that were discussed in the previous chapter, although possibly in slightly different ways.

8. Ichikawa and Jarvis (2009) also explore the similarities between philosophical thought experiments and fiction, building on David Lewis's (1978) work on "truth in fiction". Camp (2009) also provides a fascinating treatment of the role of imagination in philosophical thought experiments.

9. Interestingly, what work has been done on expert philosophical intuitions doesn't look particularly promising for proponents of the expertise defense. Studies by Schwitzgebel and Cushman (2011) and by Schultz et al. (forthcoming) seem to suggest that expert philosophical intuitions display some of the same kinds of problematic intuitional sensitivity that folk philosophical intuitions display.

10. Kauppinen (2007), Cullen (2010), and Bengson (forthcoming) also advance versions of the thickness defense.

11. Weinberg and Alexander (forthcoming) call these two kinds of conditions *veritist conditions* and *methodological conditions*, respectively. They argue that there are two important veritist conditions: an *immunity* condition – philosophical intuitions shouldn't be subject (to any worrisome degree) to the kinds of evidential diversity and problematic evidential sensitivity displayed by the kinds of mental states studied by experimental philosophers – and a *Hippocraticity* condition – philosophical intuitions shouldn't be subject (to any worrisome degree) to other kinds of problematic evidential sensitivity. They also argue that there are two important methodological conditions: a *manifestability* condition – we can tell which mental states are genuine philosophical intuitions – and a *current practice* condition – we can do this using the methods commonly associated with traditional analytic philosophy.

12. Ichikawa (forthcoming) makes the same point, arguing that it is hard to come by examples of philosophers making explicit appeal to our philosophical intuitions in philosophical discussions, except in cases where philosophers (for example, Goldman 2007) are engaged in studying human psychology, namely, our shared or individual philosophical concepts.

13. Actually, it isn't clear that Williamson would be entirely happy with this way of talking about things. Williamson's preferred reconstruction of the Gettier argument is this:

    (A) It's possible for someone to stand in relation to some proposition p just as the protagonists of Gettier's cases stand to the relevant propositions.

    (B) If someone were to stand in relation to some proposition p

just as the protagonists of Gettier's cases stand to the relevant propositions, then anyone who stood in relation to *p* just as the protagonists of Gettier's cases stand to the relevant propositions would have a justified true belief that *p* that isn't knowledge.

(C) Therefore, it is possible for someone to have a justified true belief that isn't knowledge.

Although (A) and (C) are the same as (1) and (3), it is important to note that (B) is not the same as (2). In fact, Williamson rejects something like (2) on the grounds that there are ways of filling out the details of Gettier's thought experiments such that the vignettes don't present cases of justified true beliefs that aren't knowledge. Since this point is rather controversial, and since nothing turns in what follows on which formulation we use, we can stick with (1)–(4).

14. It is important to keep in mind that when philosophers appeal to intuitions as evidence, they are not (at least typically) appealing merely to their own intuitions. Philosophical analysis is not mere intellectual autobiography and for good reason: an appeal to one's own intuitions would not be dialectically effective. For further discussion, see Alexander and Weinberg (2007).

15. Ichikawa (forthcoming) introduces an interesting distinction between different kinds of metaphilosophical claims:

(1) Intuited contents are (often) taken as important evidence/reasons/data/input in armchair philosophy.

(2) Intuited contents are (often) taken as important evidence/reasons/data/input in armchair philosophy because they are intuited.

(3) Intuition states, or facts about intuition states, are (often) taken as important evidence/reasons/data/input in armchair philosophy.

In these terms, the view being defended here is either (2) or some hybrid of (2) and (3).

16. Here, we are assuming that one of the functions of evidence is to provide an epistemic basis for our beliefs. On this view of evidence, if Williamson is right that the evidence we have for believing that (2) consists in the fact that (2), then the epistemic basis for that belief would also be the fact that (2). Although this is not one of the functions that Williamson explicitly assigns to evidence (see, e.g., Williamson 1997, 2000), nothing that he says about evidence rules out its functioning in this capacity (see, e.g., Williamson 1997, p. 728). Having said that, there are places where it seems that Williamson has a different basis in mind

for our belief that (2): namely, our "capacity for applying epistemological concepts" (Williamson 2007, p. 189). It is hard to see, however, that viewing things in this way actually helps Williamson's case against the evidentiary status of intuitions. After all, most philosophers engaged in the debate about whether or not philosophical intuitions count as evidence view this capacity precisely as the capacity for producing epistemic *intuitions*. This would make (2) a philosophical intuition (at least in the sense relevant to any debate about their evidentiary status) and would, subsequently, mean that intuition plays a direct evidentiary role in the argument for the truth of (4).

17. In addition to this worry about the dialectical standard of evidence, Williamson also claims that appealing to the dialectical nature of philosophy doesn't *favor* treating philosophical intuitions as evidence. According to Williamson, there are some contexts in which there is (or would be) controversy about what counts as a genuine philosophical intuition, what counts as the proper expression of a philosophical intuition, why philosophical intuitions should count as evidence, whether or not there are such things as philosophical intuitions, etc. (see, for example, Williamson 2004, pp. 119–123; 2007, pp. 235–237.) Of course, even if Williamson is right, the fact that there might be contexts in which we can't appeal to philosophical intuitions as evidence doesn't mean that we can never appeal to them. To support this stronger claim, Williamson would have to make the case that such problems will arise in *all* contexts. Since Williamson doesn't argue for this stronger claim, it doesn't seem like this can be reason to reject a dialectical picture of philosophy that treats philosophical intuitions as evidence.

18. We may need to adjust this revised dialectical standard somewhat to deal with people whose skeptical attitudes are local rather than global – people who deny only that certain kinds of reasons are good enough reasons for believing that *p*. The important point, however, is that we can distinguish between being unpersuaded and being (locally or globally) unpersuadable and that it seems possible to adopt a dialectical standard of evidence that doesn't require that evidence be capable of persuading the unpersuadable.

References

Adams, F. and Steadman, A. 2004a: Intentional Action in Ordinary Language: Core Concept or Pragmatic Understanding? *Analysis* 64, 173–181.

Adams, F. and Steadman, A. 2004b: Intentional Action and Moral Considerations: Still Pragmatic. *Analysis* 64, 268–276.

Alexander, J. 2010: Is Experimental Philosophy Philosophically Significant? *Philosophical Psychology* 23, 377–389.

Alexander, J. and Weinberg, J. 2007: Analytic Epistemology and Experimental Philosophy. *Philosophy Compass* 2, 56–80.

Alexander, J., Mallon, R., and Weinberg, J. 2010a: Accentuate the Negative. *Review of Philosophy and Psychology* 1, 297–314.

Alexander, J., Mallon, R., and Weinberg, J. 2010b: Competence: What's In? What's Out? Who Knows? *Behavioral and Brain Sciences* 33, 329–330.

Alicke, M. 2008: Blaming Badly. *Journal of Cognition and Culture* 8, 179–186.

Annas, J. 2003: Virtue Ethics and Social Psychology. *A Priori* 2, 20–59.

Appiah, A. 2008: *Experiments in Ethics*. Cambridge, MA: Harvard University Press.

Arico, A. 2010: Folk Psychology, Consciousness, and Context Effects. *Review of Philosophy and Psychology* 1, 371–393.

Arico, A., Fiala, B., Goldberg, R., and Nichols, S. 2011: The Folk Psychology of Consciousness. *Mind & Language* 22, 21–35.

Baron, J. 2000: *Thinking and Deciding*, 3rd edn. New York: Cambridge University Press.

Bealer, G. 1992: The Incoherence of Empiricism. *Proceedings of the Aristotelian Society* 66, 99–138.

Bealer, G. 1996a: A Priori Knowledge and the Scope of Philosophy. *Philosophical Studies* 66, 121–142.

Bealer, G. 1996b: On the Possibility of Philosophical Knowledge. *Philosophical Perspectives* 10, 1–34.

Bealer, G. 1998: Intuition and the Autonomy of Philosophy. In M. DePaul and W. Ramsey (eds.) *Rethinking Intuition*. Lanham, MD: Rowman and Littlefield, 201–240.

Beebe, J. and Buckwalter, W. 2010: The epistemic side-effect effect. *Mind & Language* 25, 474–498.

Bengson, J. Forthcoming: Experimental Attacks on Intuitions and Answers. *Philosophy and Phenomenological Research.*

Berker, S. 2009: The Normative Insignificance of Neuroethics. *Philosophy & Public Affairs* 90, 188–209.

Boghossian, P. 2006: *Fear of Knowledge: Against Relativism and Constructivism.* Oxford: Oxford University Press.

BonJour, L. 1992: A Rationalist Manifesto, *Canadian Journal of Philosophy Supplementary Volume 18*, 53–88.

BonJour, L. 1998: *In Defense of Pure Reason: A Rationalist Account of A Priori Justification.* Cambridge: Cambridge University Press.

Brown, J. Forthcoming: Experimental Philosophy, Contextualism and SSI. *Philosophy and Phenomenological Research*, doi: 10.1111/j.1933-1592.2010.00461.x

Buckwalter, W. 2010: Knowledge Isn't Closed on Saturdays. *Review of Philosophy and Psychology* 1, 395–406.

Buckwalter, W. Forthcoming: The Mystery of Stakes and Error in Ascriber Intuitions. Manuscript under review.

Buckwalter, W. and Stich, S. Forthcoming: Gender and Philosophical Intuitions. Manuscript under review.

Cacioppo, J.T. and Petty, R.E. 1982: The Need for Cognition. *Journal of Personality and Social Psychology* 42, 116–131.

Camp, E. 2009: Two Varieties of Literary Imagination: Metaphor, Fiction, and Thought Experiments. *Midwest Studies in Philosophy* 33, 107–130.

Chalmers, D. 1996: *The Conscious Mind: In Search of a Fundamental Theory.* Oxford: Oxford University Press.

Chomsky, N. 1965: *Aspects of the Theory of Syntax.* Cambridge, MA: The MIT Press.

Christensen, D. 2007: Epistemology and Disagreement: The Good News. *The Philosophical Review* 116, 187–217.

Cohen, S. 1998: Contextualist Solutions to Epistemological Problems:

Skepticism, Gettier, and the Lottery. *Australasian Journal of Philosophy* 76, 289–306.

Cokely, E. and Feltz, A. 2009: Individual Differences, Judgment Biases, and Theory-of-Mind: Deconstructing the Intentional Action Side Effect Asymmetry. *Journal of Research in Personality* 43, 18–24.

Cullen, S. 2010: Survey-Driven Romanticism. *Review of Philosophy and Psychology* 1, 275–296.

Cummins, R. 1998: Reflection on Reflective Equilibrium. In M. DePaul and W. Ramsey (eds.) *Rethinking Intuition*. Lanham, MD: Rowman and Littlefield, 113–128.

Cushman, F. and Mele, A. 2008: Intentional Action: Two-and-a-Half Folk Concepts? In J. Knobe and S. Nichols (eds.) *Experimental Philosophy*. Oxford: Oxford University Press, 171–188.

Darley, J. and Batson, C. 1973: From Jerusalem to Jericho: A Study of Situational and Dispositional Variables in Helping Behavior. *Journal of Personality and Social Psychology* 27, 100–108.

DeRose, K. 1992: Contextualism and Knowledge Attributions. *Philosophy and Phenomenological Research* 52, 172–198.

DeRose, K. 1995: Solving the Skeptical Problem. *Philosophical Review* 104, 1–52.

DeRose, K. 2011: Contextualism, Contrastivism, and X-Phi Surveys. *Philosophical Studies* 156, 81–110.

Deutsch, M. 2009: Experimental Philosophy and the Theory of Reference. *Mind & Language* 24, 445–466.

Deutsch, M. 2010: Intuitions, Counter-Examples, and Experimental Philosophy. *Review of Philosophy and Psychology* 1, 447–460.

Devitt, M. 1994: The Methodology of Naturalistic Semantics. *The Journal of Philosophy* 91, 545–572.

Devitt, M. 2006: Intuitions in Linguistics. *British Journal for the Philosophy of Science* 57, 481–513.

Devitt, M. 2010: Experimental Semantics. *Philosophy and Phenomenological Research* 82, 418–435.

Doris, J. 1998: Persons, Situations, and Virtue Ethics. *Nous* 32, 504–530.

Doris, J. 2002: *Lack of Character*. Cambridge: Cambridge University Press.

Earlenbaugh, J. and Molyneux, B. 2009a: If Intuitions Must Be Evidential Then Philosophy Is in Big Trouble. *Studia Philosophica Estonica* 2, 35–53.

Earlenbaugh, J. and Molyneux, B. 2009b: Intuitions Are Inclinations to Believe. *Philosophical Studies* 145, 89–109.

Elga, A. 2006: Reflection and Disagreement. *Nous* 41, 478–502.

Elgin, C. 1996: *Considered Judgment*. Princeton, NJ: Princeton University Press.

Ericsson, K., Charness, N., Feltovich, P., and Hoffman, R. (eds.) 2006:

The Cambridge Handbook of Expertise and Expert Performance. Cambridge: Cambridge University Press.

Fantl, J. and McGrath, M. 2002: Evidence, Pragmatics, and Justification. *The Philosophical Review* 111, 67–94.

Feldman, R. 2006: Epistemological Puzzles about Disagreement. In S. Heatherington (ed.) *Epistemology Futures.* Oxford: Oxford University Press, 216–235.

Feldman, R. and Warfield, F. 2007: *Disagreement.* Oxford: Oxford University Press.

Feltz, A. and Cokely, E. 2007: An Anomaly in Intentional Action Ascription: More Evidence of Folk Diversity. In D. McNamara and J. Trafton (eds.) *Proceedings of the 29th Annual Cognitive Science Society.* Austin, TX: Cognitive Science Society, 1748.

Feltz, A. and Cokely, E. 2009: Do Judgments About Freedom and Responsibility Depend On Who You Are? Personality Differences in Intuitions about Compatibilism and Incompatibilism. *Consciousness and Cognition* 18, 342–350.

Feltz, A. and Zarpentine, C. 2010: Do You Know More When It Matters Less? *Philosophical Psychology* 23, 683–706.

Feltz, A., Cokely, E., and Nadelhoffer, T. 2009: Natural Compatibilism versus Natural Incompatibilism: Back to the Drawing Board. *Mind & Language* 24, 1–23.

Fields, J. and Schuman, H. 1976: Public Beliefs about the Beliefs of the Public. *Public Opinion Quarterly* 40, 427–488.

Foot, P. 1967: The Problem of Abortion and the Doctrine of Double Effect. *Oxford Review* 5, 5–15.

Frankfurt, H. 1969: Alternate Possibilities and Moral Responsibility. *The Journal of Philosophy* 66, 829–839.

Gendler, T. Szabó, 2007: Philosophical Thought Experiments, Intuitions, and Cognitive Equilibrium. *Midwest Studies in Philosophy* 31, 68–89.

Gettier, E. 1963: Is Justified True Belief Knowledge? *Analysis* 23, 121–123.

Glass, A., Holyoak, K., and Santa, J. 1979: *Cognition.* Reading, MA: Addison-Wesley.

Goldman, A. 2007: Philosophical Intuitions: Their Target, Their Source, and Their Epistemic Status. *Grazer Philosophische Studien* 74, 1–26.

Goldman, A. and Pust, J. 1998: Philosophical Theory and Intuitional Evidence. In M. DePaul and W. Ramsey (eds.) *Rethinking Intuition.* Lanham, MD: Rowman and Littlefield, 179–200.

Gray, H., Gray, K., and Wegner, D. 2007: Dimensions of Mind Perception. *Science* 315, 619.

Gray, K. and Wegner, D. 2009: Moral Typecasting. *Journal of Personality and Social Psychology* 96, 505–520.

Greene, J. 2003: From Neural 'Is' to Moral 'Ought': What Are the Moral Implications of Neuroscientific Moral Psychology? *Nature Reviews Neuroscience* 4, 846–850.

Greene, J. 2008: The Secret Joke of Kant's Soul. In W. Sinnott-Armstrong (ed.) *Moral Psychology, Volume 3: The Neuroscience of Morality: Emotion, Brain Disorders, and Development*. Cambridge, MA: MIT Press, 35–80.

Greene, J., Sommerville, R., Nystrom, L., Darley, J., and Cohen, J. 2001: An fMRI Investigation of Emotional Engagement in Moral Judgment. *Science* 293, 2105–2108.

Grice, P. 1989: *Studies in the Way of Words*. Cambridge, MA: Harvard University Press.

Griffiths, P. and Stotz, K. 2006: Genes in the Postgenomic Era. *Theoretical Medicine and Bioethics* 27, 499–521.

Griffiths, P. and Stotz, K. 2007: Gene. In D. Hull and M. Ruse (eds.) *Cambridge Companion to the Philosophy of Biology*. Cambridge: Cambridge University Press, 85–102.

Grundmann, T. 2010: Some Hope for Intuitions: A Reply to Weinberg. *Philosophical Psychology* 23, 481–509.

Guglielmo, S. and Malle, B. 2009: The Timing of Blame and Intentionality: Testing the Moral Bias Hypothesis. Poster presented at the Annual Meeting of the Society for Philosophy and Psychology, Bloomington, IN.

Guglielmo, S. and Malle, B. 2010: Can Unintended Side-Effects Be Intentional? Solving a Puzzle in People's Judgments of Intentionality and Morality. *Personality and Social Psychology Bulletin* 36, 1635–1647.

Haidt, J. 2001: The Emotional Dog and Its Rationalist Tail: A Social Intuitionist Approach to Moral Judgment. *Psychological Review* 108, 814–834.

Haidt, J., Koller, S., and Dias, M. 1993: Affect, Culture and Morality. *Journal of Personality and Social Psychology* 65, 613–628.

Hales, S. 2000: The Problem of Intuition. *American Philosophical Quarterly* 37, 135–147.

Hales, S. 2006: *Relativism and the Foundations of Philosophy*. Cambridge, MA: MIT Press.

Harman, G. 1999: Moral Philosophy Meets Social Psychology: Virtue Ethics and the Fundamental Attribution Error. *Proceedings of the Aristotelian Society* 99, 315–331.

Hawthorne, J. 2004: *Knowledge and Lotteries*. Oxford: Oxford University Press.

Hawthorne, J. and Stanley, J. 2008: Knowledge and Action. *The Journal of Philosophy* 105, 571–590.

Henderson, D. and Horgan, T. 2000: What Is the A Priori and What Is It Good For? *Southern Journal of Philosophy* 38, 51–86.

Henderson, D. and Horgan, T. 2001: The A Priori Isn't All It Is Cracked Up To Be, But It Is Something. *Philosophical Topics* 29, 219–250.

Hintikka, J. 1999: The Emperor's New Intuitions. *The Journal of Philosophy* 96, 127–147.

Hitchcock, C. and Knobe, J. 2009: Cause and Norm. *The Journal of Philosophy* 106, 587–612.

Horvath, J. 2010: How (Not) to React to Experimental Philosophy. *Philosophical Psychology* 23, 447–480.

Huebner, B., Bruno, M., and Sarkissian, H. 2010: What Does the Nation of China Think about Phenomenal Consciousness? *Review of Philosophy and Psychology* 1, 225–243.

Ichikawa, J. Forthcoming: Who Needs Intuitions? Two Experimentalist Critiques. In A. Booth and D. Rowbottom (eds.) *Intuitions*. Oxford: Oxford University Press.

Ichikawa, J. and Jarvis, B. 2009: Thought-Experiment Intuitions and Truth in Fiction. *Philosophical Studies* 142: 221–246.

Ichikawa, J., Maitra, I., and Weatherson, B. Forthcoming: In Defense of a Kripkean Dogma. *Philosophy and Phenomenological Research*, doi: 10.1111/j.1933-1592.2010.00478.x.

Isen, A. and Levin, P. 1972: Effects of Feeling Good on Helping: Cookies and Kindness. *Journal of Personality and Social Psychology* 21, 384–388.

Jackman, H. 2001: Ordinary Language, Conventionalism and *a priori* Knowledge. *Dialectica* 55, 315–325.

Jackson, F. 1998a: *From Metaphysics to Ethics: A Defence of Conceptual Analysis*. Oxford: Oxford University Press.

Jackson, F. 1998b: Reference and Description Revisited. *Philosophical Perspectives* 12, 201–218.

Kamm, F. 1989: Harming Some to Save Others. *Philosophical Studies* 57, 227–60.

Kamm, F. 2007: *Intricate Ethics: Rights, Responsibilities, and Permissible Harm*. Oxford: Oxford University Press.

Kamtekar, R. 2004: Situationism and Virtue Ethics on the Content of Our Character. *Ethics* 114, 458–491.

Kane, R. 1999: Responsibility, Luck, and Chance: Reflections on Free Will and Indeterminism. *The Journal of Philosophy* 96, 217–240.

Kauppinen, A. 2007: The Rise and Fall of Experimental Philosophy. *Philosophical Explorations* 10, 95–118.

Kelly, T. 2005: The Epistemic Significance of Disagreement. In J. Hawthorne and T. Gendler Szabó (eds.) *Oxford Studies in Epistemology*, Vol. 1. Oxford: Oxford University Press, 167–196.

Kelly, T. 2007: Peer Disagreements and Higher Order Evidence. In R. Feldman and T. Warfield (eds.) *Disagreement*. Oxford: Oxford University Press, 111–174.

Kelly, T. 2008: Disagreement, Dogmatism, and Belief Polarization. *The Journal of Philosophy* 105: 611–633.

Knobe, J. 2003a: Intentional Action and Side-effects in Ordinary Language. *Analysis* 63, 190–194.

Knobe, J. 2003b: Intentional Action in Folk Psychology: An Experimental Investigation. *Philosophical Psychology* 16, 309–323.

Knobe, J. 2004a: Folk Psychology and Folk Morality: Response to Critics. *Journal of Theoretical and Philosophical Psychology* 24, 270–279.

Knobe, J. 2004b: Intention, Intentional Action, and Moral Considerations. *Analysis* 64, 181–187.

Knobe, J. 2006: The Concept of Intentional Action: A Case Study in the Uses of Folk Psychology. *Philosophical Studies* 130, 203–231.

Knobe, J. 2007a: Experimental Philosophy. *Philosophy Compass* 2, 81–92.

Knobe, J. 2007b: Experimental Philosophy and Philosophical Significance. *Philosophical Explorations* 10, 119–122.

Knobe, J. and Burra, A. 2006: Intention and Intentional Action: A Cross-Cultural Study. *Journal of Culture and Cognition* 6, 113–132.

Knobe, J. and Kelly, S. 2009: Can One Act for a Reason Without Acting Intentionally? In C. Sandis (ed.) *New Essays on the Explanation of Action*. Basingstoke: Palgrave Macmillan, 169–183.

Knobe, J. and Mendlow, G. 2004: The Good, the Bad and the Blameworthy: Understanding the Role of Evaluative Reasoning in Folk Psychology. *Journal of Theoretical and Philosophical Psychology* 24, 252–258.

Knobe, J. and Nichols, S. 2008. An Experimental Philosophy Manifesto. In J. Knobe and S. Nichols (eds.) *Experimental Philosophy*. Oxford: Oxford University Press, 3–16.

Knobe, J. and Prinz, J. 2008: Intuitions about Consciousness. *Phenomenology and the Cognitive Sciences* 1, 67–83.

Kornblith, H. 1998: The Role of Intuitions in Philosophical Inquiry: An Account with No Unnatural Ingredients. In M. DePaul and W. Ramsey (eds.) *Rethinking Intuition*. Lanham, MD: Rowman and Littlefield, 129–142.

Kornblith, H. 2002: *Knowledge and Its Place in Nature*. Oxford: Oxford University Press.

Kornblith, H. 2007: Naturalism and Intuitions. *Grazer Philosophische Studien* 72, 27–49.

Kornblith, H. 2010: What Reflective Endorsement Cannot Do. *Philosophy and Phenomenological Research* 80, 1–19.

Kripke, S. 1980: *Naming and Necessity*. Cambridge, MA: Harvard University Press.

Kupperman, J. 2001: The Indispensability of Character. *Philosophy* 76, 239–250.

Lehrer, K. 1990: *Theory of Knowledge*. Oxford: Routledge.

Leslie, A., Knobe, J., and Cohen, A. 2006: Acting Intentionally and the Side-effect Effect: Theory of Mind and Moral Judgment. *Psychological Science* 17, 421–427.

Levin, J. 2005: The Evidential Status of Philosophical Intuition. *Philosophical Studies* 121, 193–224.

Lewis, D. 1978: Truth in Fiction. *American Philosophical Quarterly* 15, 37–46. Reprinted in D. Lewis, *Philosophical Papers: Volume I*. New York: Oxford University Press.

Lewis, D. 1983: *Philosophical Papers: Volume I*. New York: Oxford University Press.

Lewis, D. 1996: Elusive Knowledge. *Australasian Journal of Philosophy* 74, 549–567.

Liao, S.M. 2008: A Defense of Intuitions. *Philosophical Studies* 140, 247–262.

Liao, S.M., Wiegmann, A., Alexander, J., and Vong, G. Forthcoming: Putting the Trolley in Order: Experimental Philosophy and the Loop Case. *Philosophical Psychology*.

Livengood, J., Sytsma, J., Feltz, A., Scheines, R., and Machery, E. 2010: Philosophical Temperament. *Philosophical Psychology* 23, 313–330.

Lombrozo, T. 2006: The Structure and Function of Explanations. *Trends in Cognitive Sciences* 10, 464–470.

Lombrozo, T. 2011: The Instrumental Value of Explanations. *Philosophy Compass* 6, 539–551.

Lombrozo, T. and Carey, S. 2006: Functional Explanation and the Function of Explanation. *Cognition* 99, 167–204.

Ludwig, K. 2007: The Epistemology of Thought Experiments: First Person versus Third Person Approaches. *Midwest Studies in Philosophy* 31, 128–159.

Ludwig, K. 2010: Intuitions and Relativity. *Philosophical Psychology*, 23, 427–445.

Lynch, M. 2006: Trusting Intuitions. In P. Greenough and M. Lynch (eds.) *Truth and Realism*. Oxford: Oxford University Press, 227–238.

Machery, E. 2008: Understanding the Folk Concept of Intentional Action: Philosophical and Experimental Issues. *Mind & Language* 2, 165–189.

Machery, E. 2010: The Bleak Implications of Moral Psychology. *Neuroethics* 3, 223–231.

Machery, E., Mallon, R., Nichols, S., and Stich, S. 2004: Semantics, Cross-Cultural Style. *Cognition* 92, B1–B12.

Malle, B. 2006: Intentionality, Morality, and their Relationship in Human Judgment. *Journal of Cognition and Culture* 6, 87–112.

Malle, B. and Nelson, S. 2003: Judging *mens rea:* The Tension between Folk Concepts and Legal Concepts of Intentionality. *Behavioral Sciences and the Law* 21, 563–580.

Mallon, R. 2009: Knobe vs. Machery: Testing the Trade-Off Hypothesis. *Mind & Language* 23, 246–255.

Mallon, R., Machery, E., Nichols, S., and Stich, S. 2009: Against Arguments from Reference. *Philosophy and Phenomenological Research* 79, 332–356.

Marr, D. 1982: *Vision: A Computational Approach.* San Francisco, CA: Freeman & Co.

Marti, G. 2009: Against Semantic Multiculturalism. *Analysis* 69, 42–48.

May, J., Sinnott-Armstrong, W., Hull, J.G., and Zimmerman, A. 2010: Practical Interests, Relevant Alternatives, and Knowledge Attributions: An Empirical Study. *Review of Philosophy and Psychology* 1, 265–273.

McCann, H. 2005: Intentional Action and Intending: Recent Empirical Studies. *Philosophical Psychology* 18: 737–748.

Mele, A. 2001: Acting Intentionally: Probing Folk Notions. In B. Malle, L. Moses, and D. Baldwin (eds.) *Intentions and Intentionality: Foundations of Social Cognition.* Cambridge, MA: MIT Press, 27–44.

Mele, A. and Cushman, F. 2007: Intentional Action, Folk Judgments, and Stories: Sorting Things Out. *Midwest Studies in Philosophy* 31, 184–201.

Milgram, S. 1974: *Obedience to Authority: An Experimental View.* New York: Harper & Row.

Monin, B. and Miller, D. 2001: Moral Credentials and the Expression of Prejudice. *Journal of Personality and Social Psychology* 81, 33–43.

Nadelhoffer, T. 2004a: On Praise, Side Effects, and Folk Ascriptions of Intentionality. *Journal of Theoretical and Philosophical Psychology* 24, 196–213.

Nadelhoffer, T. 2004b: Blame, Badness, and Intentional Action: A Reply to Knobe and Mendlow. *Journal of Theoretical and Philosophical Psychology* 24, 259–269.

Nadelhoffer, T. 2005: Skill, Luck, Control, and Intentional Action. *Philosophical Psychology* 18, 341–352.

Nadelhoffer, T. 2006a: Desire, Foresight, Intentions, and Intentional Action: Probing Folk Intuitions. *Journal of Cognition and Culture* 6, 133–157.

Nadelhoffer, T. 2006b: Bad Acts, Blameworthy Agents, and Intentional Actions: Some Problems for Juror Impartiality. *Philosophical Explorations* 9, 203–220.

Nadelhoffer, T. and Nahmias, E. 2007: The Past and Future of Experimental Philosophy. *Philosophical Explorations* 10, 123–149.

Nado, J. 2008: Effects of Moral Cognition on Judgments of Intentionality. *British Journal for the Philosophy of Science* 59, 709–731.

Nagel, J. 2007: Epistemic Intuitions. *Philosophy Compass* 2, 792–819.

Nagel, J. 2010: Knowledge Ascriptions and the Psychological Consequences of Thinking about Error. *The Philosophical Quarterly* 60, 286–306.

Nagel, J. Forthcoming: Intuitions and Experiments: A Defense of the Case Method in Epistemology. *Philosophy and Phenomenological Research*.

Nahmias, E. and Murray, D. 2011: Experimental Philosophy on Free Will: An Error Theory for Incompatibilist Intuitions. In J. Aguilar, A. Buckareff, and K. Frankish (eds.) *New Waves in Philosophy of Action*. New York: Palgrave Macmillan, 189–216.

Nahmias, E., Morris, S., Nadelhoffer, T., and Turner, J. 2004: The Phenomenology of Free Will. *Journal of Consciousness Studies* 11, 162–179.

Nahmias, E., Morris, S., Nadelhoffer, T., and Turner, J. 2005: Surveying Freedom: Folk Intuitions About Free Will and Moral Responsibility. *Philosophical Psychology* 18, 561–584.

Nahmias, E., Morris, S., Nadelhoffer, T., and Turner, J. 2006: Is Incompatibilism Intuitive? *Philosophy and Phenomenological Research* 73, 28–53.

Nahmias, E., Coates, D., and Kvaran, T. 2007: Free Will, Moral Responsibility, and Mechanism: Experiments on Folk Intuitions. *Midwest Studies in Philosophy* 31, 214–242.

Nichols, S. 2004a: Folk Concepts and Intuitions: From Philosophy to Cognitive Science. *Trends in Cognitive Sciences* 8, 514–518.

Nichols, S. 2004b: *Sentimental Rules: On the Natural Foundations of Moral Judgment*. Oxford: Oxford University Press.

Nichols, S. and Knobe, J. 2007: Moral Responsibility and Determinism: The Cognitive Science of Folk Intuitions. *Nous*, 41, 663–685.

Nichols, S. and Ulatowski, J. 2007: Intuitions and Individual Differences: The Knobe Effect Revisited. *Mind & Language* 22, 346–365.

Nichols, S., Stich, S., and Weinberg, J. 2003: Metaskepticism: Meditations in Ethno-Epistemology. In S. Luper (ed.) *The Skeptics: Contemporary Debates*. Burlington, VT: Ashgate Press, 227–248.

Nickerson, R. 1998: Confirmation Bias: A Ubiquitous Phenomenon in Many Guises. *Review of General Psychology* 2, 175–220.

Nisbett, R. 2003: *The Geography of Thought*. New York: Free Press.

Nisbett, R. and Norenzayan, A. 2002: Culture and Cognition. In H. Plasher, S. Yantis, D. Medin, R. Gallistel, and J. Waxted (eds.) *Steven's Handbook of Experimental Psychology*, 3rd edn. Hoboken, NJ: Wiley, 561–597.

Nisbett, R. and Wilson, T. 1977: Telling More than We Can Know: Verbal Reports on Mental Processes. *Psychological Review* 84, 231–259.

Nisbett, R., Peng, K., Choi, I., and Norenzayan, A. 2001: Culture and Systems of Thought: Holistic vs. Analytic Cognition. *Psychological Review* 108, 291–310.

Norton, M., Vandello, J., and Darley, J. 2004: Casuistry and Social Category Bias. *Journal of Personality and Social Psychology* 87, 817–831.

O'Connor, T. 2000: *Persons and Causes: The Metaphysics of Free Will.* New York: Oxford University Press.

Pereboom, D. 2001: *Living Without Free Will.* Cambridge: Cambridge University Press.

Petrinovich, L. and O'Neill, P. 1996: Influence of Wording and Framing Efects on Moral Intuitions. *Ethology and Sociobiology* 17, 145–171.

Pettit, D. and Knobe, J. 2009: The Pervasive Impact of Moral Judgment. *Mind & Language* 24: 586–604.

Phelan, M. Forthcoming: Evidence That Stakes Don't Matter For Evidence. Manuscript under review.

Phelan, M. and Sarkissian, H. 2009: Is the Trade-off Hypothesis Worth Trading For? *Mind & Language* 24, 164–180.

Pinillos, N.A. Forthcoming: Knowledge, Experiments, and Practical Interests. In J. Brown and M. Gerken (eds.) *New Essays On Knowledge Ascriptions.* Oxford: Oxford University Press.

Pinillos, N.A. and Simpson, S. Forthcoming: Experimental Evidence in Support of Anti-Intellectualism about Knowledge. Manuscript under review.

Pink, T. 2004: *Free Will: A Very Short Introduction.* New York: Oxford University Press.

Plant, E. and Devine, P. 1998: Internal and External Sources of Motivation to Respond without Prejudice. *Journal of Personality and Social Psychology* 75, 811–832.

Plantinga, A. 1993: *Warrant and Proper Function.* Oxford: Oxford University Press.

Prinz, J. 2007: *The Emotional Construction of Morals.* Oxford: Oxford University Press.

Pronin, E., Lin, D., and Ross, L. 2002: The Bias Blindspot: Perceptions of Bias in Self Versus Others. *Personality and Social Psychology Bulletin* 28, 369–381.

Pust, J. 2000: *Intuitions as Evidence.* New York: Garland Publishing.

Pylyshyn, Z. 1984: *Computation and Cognition.* Cambridge, MA: MIT Press.

Robbins, P. and Jack, A. 2006: The Phenomenal Stance. *Philosophical Studies* 127, 59–85.

Rorty, R. 1967: *The Linguistic Turn.* Chicago, IL: University of Chicago Press.

Roskies, A. and Nichols, S. 2008: Bringing Moral Responsibility Down To Earth. *The Journal of Philosophy* 105, 371–388.

Ross, L. 1977: The False Consensus Effect: An Egocentric Bias in Social Perception and Attribution Processes. *Journal of Experimental Social Psychology* 13, 279–301.

Roxborough, C. and Cumby, J. 2009: Folk Psychological Concepts: Causation. *Philosophical Psychology* 22, 205–213.

Schaffer, J. 2005: Contrastive Knowledge. *Oxford Studies in Epistemology* 1, 235–271.

Schaffer, J. and Knobe, J. 2011: Contrastive Knowledge Surveyed. *Nous*, doi: 10.1111/j.1468-0068.2010.00795.x.

Schultz, E., Cokely, E., and Feltz, A. Forthcoming: Persistent Bias in Expert Judgments about Free Will and Moral Responsibility: A Test of the Expertise Defense. *Consciousness and Cognition*.

Schwarz, N. 1995: What Respondents Learn from Questionnaires: The Survey Interview and the Logic of Conversation. *International Statistical Review/Revue Internationale de Statistique* 63, 153–168.

Schwarz, N. 1996: *Cognition and Communication: Judgment Biases, Research Methods, and the Logic of Conversation.* Mahwah, NJ: Erlbaum.

Schwitzgebel, E. 2009: Do Ethicists Steal More Books? *Philosophical Psychology* 22, 711–725.

Schwitzgebel, E. and Cushman, F. 2012: Expertise in Moral Reasoning? Order Effects on Moral Judgment in Professional Philosophers and Non-Philosophers. *Mind & Language*, forthcoming.

Schwitzgebel, E. and Rust, J. 2009: The Moral Behavior of Ethicists: Peer Opinion. *Mind* 118, 1043–1059.

Schwitzgebel, E. and Rust, J. 2010: Do Ethicists and Political Philosophers Vote More Often Than Other Professors? *Review of Philosophy and Psychology* 1, 189–199.

Schwitzgebel, E. and Rust, J. Forthcoming: The Self-Reported Behavior of Ethics Professors. Manuscript under review.

Schwitzgebel, E., Rust, J., Huang, L., Moore, A., and Coates, J. Forthcoming: Ethicists' Courtesy at Philosophy Conferences. *Philosophical Psychology*.

Shanteau, J. 1992: Competence in Experts: The Role of Task Characteristics. *Organizational Behavior and Human Decision Processes* 53, 252–266.

Singer, P. 1972: Moral Experts. *Analysis* 32, 115–117.

Singer, P. 1982: How Do We Decide? *The Hastings Center Report* 12, 9–11.

Singer, P. 2005: Ethics and Intuitions. *Journal of Ethics* 9, 331–352.

Sinnott-Armstrong, W. 2008: Framing Moral Intuitions. In W. Sinnott-Armstrong (ed.) *Moral Psychology, Volume 2: The Cognitive Science of Morality.* Cambridge, MA: MIT Press, 47–76.

Sommers, T. 2010: Experimental Philosophy and Free Will. *Philosophy Compass* 5, 199–212.

Sommers, T. 2011: In Memoriam: The X-Phi Debate. *The Philosophers' Magazine* 52, 89–93.

Sosa, E. 1991: *Knowledge in Perspective: Selected Essays in Epistemology.* Cambridge: Cambridge University Press.

Sosa, E. 1996: Rational Intuition: Bealer on Its Nature and Epistemic Status. *Philosophical Studies* 81, 151–162.

Sosa, E. 1998: Minimal Intuition. In M. DePaul and W. Ramsey (eds.) *Rethinking Intuition.* Lanham, MD: Rowman and Littlefield, 257–270.

Sosa, S. 2007a: Experimental Philosophy and Philosophical Intuition. *Philosophical Studies* 132, 99–107.

Sosa, E. 2007b: Intuitions: Their Nature and Epistemic Efficacy. *Grazer Philosophische Studien* 74, 51–67.

Sosa, E. 2009: A Defense of the Use of Intuitions in Philosophy. In M. Bishop and D. Murphy (eds.) *Stich and His Critics.* Malden, MA: Wiley-Blackwell, 101–112.

Sreenivasan, G. 2002: Errors about Errors: Virtue Theory and Trait Attribution. *Mind* 111, 47–68.

Stalnaker, R. 1999: *Context and Content*, Oxford: Oxford University Press.

Stanley, J. 2005: *Knowledge and Practical Interests.* Oxford: Oxford University Press.

Starmans, C. and Friedman, O. Forthcoming: A Sex Difference in Adults' Attributions of Knowledge. Manuscript under review.

Stich, S. 1988: Reflective Equilibrium, Analytic Epistemology and the Problem of Cognitive Diversity. *Synthese* 74, 391–413.

Stich, S. 1990: *The Fragmentation of Reason: Preface to a Pragmatic Theory of Cognitive Evaluation.* Cambridge, MA: MIT Press.

Stich, S. and Buckwalter, W. 2011: Gender and the Philosophy Club. *The Philosopher's Magazine* 52, 60–65.

Stich, S. and Nisbett, R. 1980: Justification and the Psychology of Human Reasoning. *Philosophy of Science* 47, 188–202.

Strawson, G. 1986: *Freedom and Belief.* New York: Oxford University Press.

Swain, S., Alexander, J., and Weinberg, J. 2008: The Instability of Philosophical Intuitions: Running Hot and Cold on Truetemp. *Philosophy and Phenomenological Research* 76, 138–155.

Sytsma, J. and Livengood, J. 2011: A New Perspective Concerning Experiments on Semantic Intuitions. *Australasian Journal of Philosophy* 89, 315–332.

Sytsma, J. and Machery, E. 2010: Two Conceptions of Subjective Experience. *Philosophical Studies* 151, 299–327.

Talbot, B. 2009: Psychology and the Use of Intuitions in Philosophy. *Studia Philosophica Estonia* 2, 157–176.

Thomson, J. 1985: The Trolley Problem. *The Yale Law Journal* 94, 1395–1415.

Tversky, A. and Kahneman, D. 1974: Judgment under Uncertainty: Heuristics and Biases. *Science* 185, 1124–1131. Reprinted in D. Kahneman, P. Slovic, and A. Tversiky (eds.) *Judgment Under Uncertainty: Heuristics and Biases.* Cambridge: Cambridge University Press.

Uhlmann, E., Pizarro, D., Tannenbaum, D., and Ditto, P. 2009: The Motivated Use of Moral Principles. *Judgment and Decision Making* 4, 476–491.

van Inwagen, P. 1997: Materialism and the Psychological-Continuity Account of Personal Identity. *Nous* 31, 305–319.

Wason, P. 1960: On the Failure to Eliminate Hypotheses in a Conceptual Task. *The Quarterly Journal of Experimental Psychology* 12, 129–140.

Weatherson, B. 2003: What Good Are Counterexamples? *Philosophical Studies* 115, 1–31.

Weatherson, B. Forthcoming: Defending Interest-Relative Invariantism. Manuscript under review.

Weinberg, J. 2007: How To Challenge Intuitions Empirically Without Risking Skepticism. *Midwest Studies in Philosophy* 31, 318–343.

Weinberg, J. and Alexander, J. Forthcoming: The Challenge of Sticking with Intuitions through Thick and Thin. In A. Booth and D. Rowbottom (eds.) *Intuitions.* Oxford: Oxford University Press.

Weinberg, J., Nichols, S., and Stich, S. 2001: Normativity and Epistemic Intuitions. *Philosophical Topics* 29, 429–460.

Weinberg, J., Gonnerman, C., Buckner, C., and Alexander, J. 2010: Are Philosophers Expert Intuiters? *Philosophical Psychology* 23, 331–355.

Weinberg, J., Alexander, J., Gonnerman, C., and Reuter, S. Forthcoming: Restrictionism & Reflection: Challenge Deflected, or Simply Redirected? *The Monist.*

White, R. 2005. Epistemic Permissiveness. *Philosophical Perspectives* 19, 445–459.

Williamson, T. 1997: Knowledge as Evidence. *Mind* 106, 717–741.

Williamson, T. 2000: *Knowledge and Its Limits.* Oxford: Oxford University Press.

Williamson, T. 2004: Philosophical 'Intuitions' and Scepticism about Judgment. *Dialectica* 58, 109–155.

Williamson, T. 2005: Armchair Philosophy, Metaphysical Modality and Counterfactual Thinking. *Proceedings of the Aristotelian Society* 105, 1–23.

Williamson, T. 2007: *The Philosophy of Philosophy.* Oxford: Blackwell Publishing.

Williamson, T. 2011: Philosophical Expertise and the Burden of Proof. *Metaphilosophy* 42, 215–229.

Wilson, T. 2002: *Strangers to Ourselves: Discovering the Adaptive Unconscious.* Cambridge, MA: Harvard University Press.

Wright, J. 2010: On Intuitional Stability: The Clear, the Strong, and the Paradigmatic. *Cognition* 115, 419–503.

Young, L., Cushman, F., Adolphs, R., Tranel, D., and Hauser, M. 2006: Does Emotion Mediate the Effect of an Action's Moral Status on Its Intentional Status? Neuropsychological Evidence. *Journal of Cognition and Culture* 6, 291–304.

Zamzow, J. and Nichols, S. 2009: Variations in Ethical Intuitions. *Philosophical Issues* 19, 368–388.

Index

abstract 23, 31–2, 117 n.14, 118 n.6,
    122 n.1,
Adams, F. 54–6
affect 3, 6, 30–7, 58–60, 78–9, 82–3, 95,
    111, 118 n.3, n.6, 119 n.19, 123
    n.10, 123–4 n.11, 124 n.12, n.16,
    130 n.18
Alexander, J. 20, 24, 79, 94, 96, 98–9,
    103, 111, 114 n.1, 115 n.4, 116
    n.9, n.10, 117 n.15, 118 n.7, 119
    n.11, 125 n.17, 132 n.11, 133 n.14
Alicke, M. 122 n.4
American car case 72–3, 127 n.2
Annas, J. 5
anti-intellectualism 41
Appiah, A. 5
Arico, A. 4

bank cases
    concrete high standard case 45–6
    DeRose bank cases 36–8
    high stakes alternative case 40
    high stakes case 41–2
    high stakes no alternative case 40
    high stakes typo case 46–7
    high standards case 39
    important case 43–4
    low stakes case 41–2

low stakes typo case 46–7
low standards case 38–9
revised low standard case 45–6
simplified high stakes case 42–3
simplified low stakes case 42–3
unimportant case 43–4
Baron, J. 97
Batson, C. 5
Bealer, G. 11, 18–19, 21, 24, 114 n.1,
    115 n.7, 116 n.11, 117 n.12
Beebe, J. 69
Bengson, J. 116 n.11, 132 n.10
Berker, S. 7
blame 54–7, 59–60, 117 n.2, 124 n.12,
    n.14, n.15, n.16
Boghossian, P. 119 n.13, 130 n.18
BonJour, L. 116 n.11
Brown, J. 121 n.26
Buckner, C. 94
Buckwalter, W. 38–40, 46–7, 69, 74–6,
    120 n.22
Burra, A. 122 n.3
button case 80–1, 130 n.19

Cacioppo, J. 119 n.16
Camp, E. 132 n.8
Carey, S. 8
caring lieutenant case 65–6

car thief case 58–9, 124 n.12
causal theory of reference 14–16
causation 69
Chalmers, D. 115 n.5
character 5
child case 75, 127 n.5
Chomsky, N. 60, 101
Christensen, D. 119 n.12
Cohen, S. 119 n.16, n.17, 130 n.18
Cokely, E. 33, 128 n.8
compatibilism 16, 29–36, 118 n.3
concepts 2–3, 6, 8–9, 19, 24–5, 33–5,
    50–1, 54, 66–9, 77, 84–5, 87, 90–4,
    98–9, 115 n.2, n.7, 121–2 n.1,
    122–3 n.6, 131 n.3, 132 n.12, 133
    n.16
conceptual analysis 51
conceptual competence/performance
    24–5, 32–3, 51, 60–1, 69, 93–4,
    98–9
concrete 23, 31–2, 45–6, 118 n.6, 121
    n.27
consciousness 4–5
contextualism 36–48, 120 n.22, 121
    n.26, 130 n.18
contrastivism 46
conversational implicature 54, 122 n.5
conversational pragmatics 54–7,
    111–12
Cullen, S. 111–12, 132 n.10
Cumby, J. 69
Cummins, R. 70, 85
Cushman, F. 67–8, 122 n.3, 130 n.17,
    132 n.9

Darley, J. 5
DeRose, K. 36, 119 n.17, 120 n.22,
    130 n.18
descriptivist theory of reference 14–16,
    115 n.5
determined killer case 76
determinism 16, 29–36, 78, 117–18
    n.2, 118 n.3, 119 n.4
Deutsch, M. 101, 127 n.3
Devine, P. 79
Devitt, M. 70, 85, 130 n.1
Ditto, P. 78
doctrine of double effect 17–18, 115
    n.6
dog case 63–4, 125 n.20

Doris, J. 5
drunk driver case 56, 60
dual process theory 7

Elga, A. 119 n.12
Elgin, C. 70, 85
emotionism 6
environmental harm case 52, 54–5, 58, 62,
    66–8, 122 n.2, 123 n.7
environmental help case 52, 55, 62, 66–8,
    122 n.2, 122–3 n.6, 123 n.7
Ericsson, K. 91
Erlenbaugh, J. 116 n.8
expertise defense 90–8
explanation 8–9
extra dollar case 62–3, 125 n.18

Fantl, J. 119 n.16, n.18, 120 n.23
fat man case 78, 129 n.15
Feldman, R. 119 n.12
Feltz, A. 33–4, 42–3, 120 n.24, 128 n.8
Fields, J. 2
folk psychology 4, 69, 122 n.4
Foot, P. 115 n.6
Frankfurt, H. 16–17
free cup case 62, 125 n.19
free will 16, 29–36, 117–18 n.22
Friedman, O. 75, 127–8 n.6

Gendler, T. 114 n.1
gene 8–9
Gettier, E. 12–13
Gettier cases 12–13, 19, 103–4, 115 n.3,
    132 n.13
Glass, A. 118 n.8, 118–19 n.9
Gödel case 15–16, 23, 73–4
Goldman, A. 20, 50, 76–7, 86, 101,
    115 n.2, 121–2 n.1, 131 n.2, 132
    n.12
Gonnerman, C. 94
Gray, H. 4
Gray, K. 4
Greene, J. 7
Grice, P. 122 n.5
Griffiths, P. 9
Grundmann, T. 130 n.1
Guglielmo, S. 60, 124 n.15

habitual tax cheat case 34
Haidt, J. 6, 126 n.1

Hales, S. 90, 116 n.11, 119 n.13, 130 n.18, 130 n.1
Harman, G. 5
harmful terrorist case 64–5, 126 n.23
Hawthorne, J. 119 n.18, 120 n.23, 121 n.30
helpful terrorist case 65, 126 n.23
Henderson, D. 24
Hintikka, J. 101
Hitchcock, C. 69
Holtzman, G. 76
Horgan, T. 24
Horvath, J. 130 n.1
Huebner, B. 4
Hull, J. 40

Ichikawa, J. 101, 127 n.3, 132 n.8, 132 n.12, 133 n.15
incompatibilism 16, 29–36
intentional action 52–68, 122 n.2, n.3, 122–3 n.6, 123 n.8, n.10, 123–4 n.11, 124 n.13, n.14, n.15, n.16, 125 n.18, n.19, n.20, 126 n.23, n.24, n.25, 131 n.4
interest-relevant invariantism 119 n.18
intuitional diversity 72–7
    cultural diversity 72–4
    gender differences 74–7
intuitional sensitivity 77–81
intuitions *see* philosophical intuitions
Isen, A. 5

Jack, A. 4
Jackman, H. 131 n.2
Jackson, F. 115 n.5
Jarvis, B. 132 n.8

Kamm, F. 115 n.6
Kamtekar, R. 5
Kane, R. 117 n.1
Kauppinen, A. 24–5, 96–7, 112, 132 n.10
Kelly, S. 126 n.23
Kelly, T. 119 n.12
Knobe, J. 4, 30–4, 44–7, 52–8, 60–1, 68–9, 78, 93, 114 n.2, 118 n.6, 122 n.2, n.3, n.4, 123 n.9, 124 n.14, 125 n.18, n.21, 125–6, n.21, 126 n.23, 131 n.2

knowledge 12–13, 19–20, 23, 28, 29, 36–48, 51, 69, 77, 79–80, 82, 92–3, 97, 102–3, 105, 115 n.3, 119 n.19, 120 n.22, 120–1 n.24, 121 n.26, n.27, n.29, n.30, 121–2 n.1, 129 n.13, 131 n.13
Kornblith, H. 11, 25–6, 70, 84–5, 92, 94–6, 114–5 n.1, 117 n.15, 131 n.6
Kripke, S. 15, 73–4
Kupperman, J. 5

Lehrer, K. 14, 79
Leslie, A. 122 n.3
Levin, J. 19
Levin, P. 5
Lewis, D. 20, 103, 119 n.17, 130 n.18, 132 n.8
Liao, M. 114 n.1, 115 n.6, 130 n.17
Livengood, J. 127 n.3, 131 n.5
Lombrozo, T. 8–9
Ludwig, K. 22, 24, 90, 99, 117 n.14, 127 n.3, 131 n.1, n.3, n.4
Lynch, M. 22, 24, 95, 115

McCann, H. 122 n.3
McGrath, M. 119 n.16, n.18, 120 n.23
Machery, E. 4–5, 54, 60–4, 73, 127 n.3
Malle, B. 56, 60, 122 n.3, 123 n.8, n.10, 124 n.15
Mallon, R. 64–5, 73, 126 n.22, n.23
Marr, D. 118 n.8, 118–19 n.9
Marti, G. 127 n.3
May, J. 40, 46
Mele, A. 67–8, 122 n.3, 123 n.9
Mendlow, G. 122 n.3, 124 n.14
Milgram, S. 5
Miller, D. 79
Molyneux, B. 116 n.8
Monin, B. 79
moral judgment 6–7, 54, 57, 60–1, 122 n.4, 130 n.17
moral psychology 5–8
moral responsibility 12, 16–17, 28–36, 48, 78, 82, 117–18 n.2, 118 n.3, n.4, n.5, n.6, 119 n.10, n.14
Morris, S. 29
multiple concepts view 34–5
murderous husband case 32, 118 n.5
Murray, D. 119 n.14

Nadelhoffer, T. 29, 33, 54, 57–61, 114 n.1, n.2, 122 n.3, n.4, 123–4 n.11, 124 n.12
Nado, J. 122 n.4
Nagel, J. 114 n.1, 121 n.27
Nahmias, E. 29–30, 32, 114 n.1, n.2, 117–18 n.2, 118 n.3, 119 n.14
Nelson, S. 123 n.10
neuroethics 7
Nichols, S. 6, 30–4, 54, 66–7, 72, 74–5, 78, 93, 114 n.2, 118 n.3, n.6, 127 n.5, 128 n.9, 128 n.10, 130 n.17, 131 n.2
Nickerson, R. 97
Nisbett, R. 24, 96, 126 n.1, 130 n.1
Norenzayan, A. 126 n.1
normative 6–7, 17, 19, 35, 51–2, 57, 66, 68–9, 125 n.18, 130 n.18
Norton, M. 79
no skill/immoral outcome case 53, 56, 122 n.3
no skill/positive outcome case 53, 122 n.3

O'Connor, T. 117 n.1
O'Neill, P. 80–1, 130 n.17
order effects 3, 79–81, 129 n.13

Pereboom, D. 117 n.1
performance error *see* conceptual competence/performance
Petrinovich, L. 80–1, 130 n.17
Pettit, P. 68, 122 n.4
Petty, R. 129 n.13
Phelan, M. 43–4, 65–6, 125 n.18, 125–6 n.21, 126 n.22, n.25
philosophical analysis 2, 28–49, 115 n.4
philosophical intuitions 11–27, 89–108
  doxastic conception 20–1
  etiological conception 24
  methodological conception 25
  phenomenological conception 21–23
  semantic conception 23
philosophical methodology 3, 19–20, 70–89, 101, 109, 111, 129 n.14
philosophy of mind 3, 50–69, 84
Pinillos, N. A. 44, 46–7, 121 n.29
Pink, T. 117 n.1

Pizarro, D. 78
Plant, E. 79
Plantinga, A. 116 n.11
police officer case 58–9, 124 n.12
pragmatics *see* conversational pragmatics
praise 118 n.2, 122–3 n.6
principle of alternative possibilities 16–17
Prinz, J. 4, 6
Pronin, E. 97
push case 80–1, 129 n.16
Pust, J. 22, 86, 115 n.7, 121–2 n.1
Pylyshyn, Z. 118 n.8, 118–19 n.9

reflection 7–8, 24–5, 96–7, 107
reflective equilibrium 130 n.1
relativism 35, 77, 119 n.13, 130 n.18
restrictionist challenge 70–89
Robbins, P. 4
Rorty, R. 113
Roskies, A. 118 n.3
Ross, L. 2
Roxborough, C. 69
Rust, J. 8

salience 29, 36–48, 119 n.19, 120 n.20, 121 n.26, n.27
Sarkissian, H. 65–6, 125 n.18, 125–6 n.21, 126 n.22, n.25
Schaffer, J. 37, 44–7
Schultz, E. 132 n.9
Schuman, H. 2
Schwarz, N. 111
Schwitzgebel, E. 8, 130 n.17, 132 n.9
sentiments 6
serial rapist case 34
Shanteau, J. 91
side-effect effect 52–69, 123 n.8, 125 n.18
Simpson, S. 121 n.29
Singer, P. 7, 91, 130 n.1
Sinnott-Armstrong, W. 40, 129 n.14
situationism 5
skepticism 21, 85–7, 102–3, 105, 107, 111, 134–5 n.18
Sommers, T. 114 n.2, 119 n.15
Sosa, E. 23–4, 83, 96–7, 110, 114 n.1, 115–16 n.7, 116 n.8, 116–17 n.11, 117 n.13

Sreenivasan, G. 5
stakes 29, 36–48, 119 n.19, 120 n.21, 120–1 n.24, 121 n.26, n.28, n.29, n.31
Stalnaker, R. 115 n.5
Stanley, J. 41, 119 n.18, 121 n.30
Starmans, C. 75, 127–8 n.6
Steadman, A. 54–6
Stich, S. 72, 74–6, 130 n.1
Stotz, K. 9
stranger case 74–5, 127 n.5
Strawson, G. 117 n.1
subject-sensitive invariantism 36–48, 121 n.26
supercomputer case 29–30, 117–18 n.2
Swain, S. 79
switch case 80–1, 130 n.15
Sytsma, J. 4, 127 n.3

Talbot, B. 116 n.11
Tannenbaum, D. 78
thickness defense 99–100
Thomson, J. 17–18, 78, 115 n.6
trade-off hypothesis 62, 64, 125 n.18, 126 n.25
transplant case 18
trolley problem 7, 17–18, 63–4, 74–5, 78–9, 80–1, 115 n.6, 127 n.5, 130 n.17
Truetemp case 13–14, 79–81, 129 n.13

Tsu Ch'ung Chih case 73–4
Turner, J. 29

Uhlmann, E. 78, 128 n.11, 129 n.12
Ulatowski, J. 54, 66–7

van Inwagen, P. 21

Warfield, T. 119 n.12
Wason, P. 97
watch case 75
Weatherson, B. 115 n.3, 121 n.31
Wegner, D. 4
Weinberg, J. 20, 72, 77, 79, 83, 91, 94, 96, 98–9, 111, 114 n.1, 115 n.4, 116 n.10, 117 n.15, 129 n.13, 130 n.1, 131 n.7, n.11, 133 n.14
White, R. 119 n.12
Williamson, T. 21, 97, 102–5, 114–15 n.1, 115–16 n.7, 116 n.9, 117 n.13, 130 n.1, 132 n.13, 133 n.16, 134 n.17
Wilson, T. 24, 96, 131 n.6
worker case 63–4, 125 n.20
Wright, J. 129 n.13

Young, L. 122 n.3

Zamzow, J. 74–5, 127 n.5, 128 n.9, 128 n.10, 130 n.17
Zarpentine, C. 42–3, 120–1 n.24
Zimmerman, A. 40